cocktails AND PUNCHES

cocktails AND PUNCHES

Sophisticated Drinks for Every Occasion

Linda Doeser

Photography by Chris Linton

This is a Parragon Publishing Book
This edition published in 2004

Parragon Publishing
Queen Street House
4 Queen Street
Bath BA1 1HE, UK

Created and produced for Parragon Publishing by
The Bridgewater Book Company Limited

Creative Director Steve Knowlden
Art Director Tony Seddon
Editorial Director Fiona Biggs
Senior Editor Lorraine Turner
Editorial Assistant Tom Kitch
Photography Chris Linton
Illustrations Ian Mitchell
Studio Manager Chris Morris
Mac Artwork Loraine Hayes

ISBN 1-40541-110-4

Printed in China

NOTE Recipes using uncooked eggs should be avoided by infants, the elderly,
pregnant women, convalescents, and anyone suffering from an illness.

Contents

Introduction

Precisely where the word "cocktail" came from is uncertain. A popular piece of folklore describes how a Mexican princess called Xoctl offered a mixed drink to an American visitor to her father's court, who confused her name with that of the drink itself. Another suggestion is that the spoon used for mixing drinks reminded imbibing racegoers of the docked tails of nonthoroughbred horses, called cocktails. There are many other flights of fancy, but modern etymologists mostly agree that the word derives from *coquetel*, a French, wine-based drink.

Whatever the origins of the word cocktail, mixed drinks have existed since ancient times and the first

recognizable cocktail dates from about the sixteenth century. Indeed, many classics have been around for much longer than most people think. The bourbon-based Old Fashioned, for example, first appeared at the end of the eighteenth century.

We know that the word cocktail was already in use in 1809 in the United States and, thirty-five years later, when Charles Dickens described Major Pawkins as able to drink "more rum-toddy, mint-julep, gin-sling, and cock-tail, than any private gentleman of his acquaintance," it had reached Britain, too. Popular among the style-conscious and wealthy in the United States, cocktails were served

before dinner in the most exclusive houses and hotels until World War I made them unfashionable. They have gone in and out of vogue ever since.

Following the war, young people, disillusioned by the elder generation and desperately seeking new experiences, pleasures, stimuli, and styles, developed a taste for a new range of cocktails. Ironically, Prohibition in the United States in the 1920s spurred on their development. Illegally produced liquor frequently tasted poisonous—and sometimes was—so its flavor needed to be disguised with fruit juices and mixers. No doubt, the naughtiness of drinking alcoholic cocktails also added to their appeal to the "bright young things"

of the time. The craze quickly crossed the Atlantic and the best hotels in London, Paris, and Monte Carlo, where the quality of gin and whisky was more consistent, soon boasted their own cocktail bars.

World War II brought an end to such revelry and, although drunk occasionally, cocktails remained out of style for decades until an exuberant renaissance in the 1970s. This resulted in another new generation of recipes, often featuring white rum and vodka, and tequila, which was just becoming known outside its native Mexico. Inevitably, the pendulum swung against cocktails again until recently. Now, once more, the cocktail shaker is essential equipment in every fashionable city bar.

Essentials

MAKING, SERVING—AND, ABOVE ALL, DRINKING—COCKTAILS SHOULD BE FUN. ALL YOU NEED IS SOME BASIC EQUIPMENT, A FEW INGREDIENTS, AND A SENSE OF ADVENTURE.

EQUIPMENT

Classic cocktails are either shaken or stirred. A shaker is an essential piece of equipment, consisting of a container with an inner, perforated lid and an outer lid. Both lids are secured while the mixture is shaken, together with cracked ice, and then the cocktail is strained through the perforated lid into a glass.

A mixing glass is a medium-sized pitcher in which stirred cocktails can be mixed. It is usually made of uncolored glass so you can see what you are doing.

A long-handled bar spoon is perfect for stirring and a small strainer prevents the ice cubes—used during mixing—finding their way into the cocktail glass. Some modern cocktails, including slushes, are made in a blender or food processor, so if you have one, by all means make use of it. Any cocktail that is made by shaking in a cocktail shaker can also be made in a blender.

Measuring cups, sometimes called "jiggers," and spoons are essential for getting the proportions right—guessing does not work. A corkscrew, bottle-opener, and sharp knife are crucial.

Other useful, but nonessential tools include a citrus reamer, an ice bucket and tongs, a punch bowl, a glass serving pitcher, and a zester or grater. If you have a juicer, this is useful for making large quantities of fresh juice for cocktails.

GLASSES

You can serve cocktails in any glasses you like. Small, V-shaped, stemmed glasses may be worth buying, but it is not essential to have a full range of Old-fashioned, Highball, Collins glasses, and so on. Tumblers, small tumblers, and wine glasses cover most contingencies. As part of their appeal is

visual, cocktails are best served in clear, uncut glass. Chill the glasses in the refrigerator to ensure cocktails are cold.

INGREDIENTS

You can stock your bar over a period of time with the basics—it is not necessary to buy everything at once. A good, all-round selection of alcoholic drinks would include whisky, possibly Scotch and bourbon, brandy, gin, light and dark rum, triple sec, sweet and dry vermouth, vodka, and tequila. You could also include Pernod, beer, and red and white wine. Keep champagne cocktails for special occasions. Select your stock according to your tastes—for example, if you never drink whisky, it would be extravagant to buy Scotch, Irish, Canadian, American blended, and bourbon.

Standard mixers include club soda, sparkling mineral water, cola, ginger ale, and tonic water. Freshly squeezed fruit juice is best, but when buying juice in a bottle or carton, avoid any with added sugar or extra "padding." Cranberry juice, for example, may often be bulked out with grape juice. Commercial brands of grapefruit, orange, cranberry, tomato juice, and lime cordial are also useful to the cocktail maker.

A good supply of fresh lemons, limes, and oranges is also essential. Fresh fruit is best, but if you use canned, buy it in natural juice rather than syrup, and drain well. Other useful garnishes and condiments include Angostura bitters, Worcestershire sauce, and cocktail cherries. Finally, you can never have too much ice.

Techniques

CRACKING AND CRUSHING ICE

Store ice in the freezer until just before use. Cracked ice is used in both shaken and stirred cocktails. To crack ice, put ice cubes into a strong plastic bag and hit it against an outside wall, or put the ice between clean cloths on a sturdy surface and crush with a wooden mallet or rolling pin. Crushed ice is used in cocktails made in a blender. To crush ice, crack it as before but break it into much smaller pieces.

FROSTING GLASSES

Glasses can be frosted with sugar—or fine or coarse salt in the case of the Margarita or Salty Dog. Simply rub the rim of the glass with a wedge of lemon or lime, then dip the rim into a saucer of superfine sugar or fine salt until it is evenly coated.

Techniques

MAKING SUGAR SYRUP

To make sugar syrup, put 4 tablespoons water and 4 tablespoons superfine sugar into a small pan and stir over a low heat until the sugar has dissolved. Bring to a boil, then continue to boil, without stirring, for 1–2 minutes. Cool, then refrigerate in a covered container for up to 2 weeks. This is used in a great many popular cocktail recipes, so it is worth having some to hand.

SHAKEN OR STIRRED?

To make a shaken cocktail, put fresh cracked ice into a cocktail shaker and pour over the other ingredients immediately. Secure the lids and shake vigorously for 10–20 seconds, until the outside of the shaker is coated in condensation. Strain into a glass and serve at once. To make a stirred cocktail, again use fresh cracked ice and pour over the ingredients immediately. Using a long-handled spoon, stir vigorously, without splashing, for 20 seconds, then strain into a glass and serve at once.

Classic Cocktails

classic cocktail

It cannot lay claim to being the first or even the only classic, but it has all the characteristic hallmarks of sophistication associated with cocktails.

SERVES 1

wedge of lemon, 1 tsp superfine sugar, 4–6 cracked ice cubes,

2 measures brandy, ½ measure clear Curaçao, ½ measure Maraschino,

½ measure lemon juice, lemon peel twist, to decorate

1 Rub the rim of a chilled cocktail glass with the lemon wedge and then dip in the sugar to frost.

2 Put the cracked ice into a cocktail shaker. Pour the brandy, Curaçao, Maraschino, and lemon juice over the ice and shake vigorously until a frost forms.

3 Strain into the frosted glass and decorate with the lemon twist.

VARIATIONS

A number of cocktails are the quintessential classics of their type and named simply after the main ingredient.

CHAMPAGNE COCKTAIL: place a sugar cube in the bottom of a chilled champagne flute and dash with Angostura bitters to douse it. Fill the glass with chilled champagne and decorate with a twist of lemon.

TEQUILA COCKTAIL: put 4–6 cracked ice cubes into a cocktail shaker. Dash Angostura bitters over the ice and pour in 3 measures golden tequila, 1 measure lime juice, and ½ measure grenadine. Shake vigorously until a frost forms, then strain into a chilled cocktail glass.

BARTENDER'S TIP

Maraschino is a sweet Italian liqueur made from cherries. It is usually white, but may also be colored red. The white version is better for most cocktails, because it does not affect the appearance of the finished drink.

boiler maker

Originally, boilermaker was slang for a shot of whiskey followed by a beer chaser. This version is marginally more sophisticated, but every bit as lethal.

SERVES 1

1 cup English Pale Ale,

1½ measures bourbon or rye whiskey

1 Pour the beer into a chilled beer glass or tankard. Pour the bourbon or rye whiskey into a chilled shot glass.

2 Gently submerge the shot glass in the beer.

VARIATIONS

DEPTH CHARGE: pour 2 measures of schnapps—choose your favorite flavor—into a chilled beer glass or tankard, then pour in 2 cups English Pale Ale.

SUBMARINO: pour 1 cup Mexican beer into a chilled beer glass or tankard. Pour 2 measures white tequila into a chilled shot glass, then gently submerge the shot glass in the beer.

YORSH: pour 1 cup English Pale Ale into a chilled beer glass or tankard, then pour in 2 measures vodka.

GINGER BEER: pour 1 cup dark beer into a chilled beer glass or tankard, then pour in 2 measures ginger brandy.

DOG'S NOSE: pour 1 cup English Pale Ale into a chilled beer glass or tankard, then pour in 1 measure gin.

BARTENDER'S TIP

You can use your favorite beer for making any of these drinks, although certain types are traditional for making particular cocktails.

french 75

Although this cocktail was described in a cocktails book written in the early twentieth century as something that "definitely hits the spot," there seems to be some confusion about the actual ingredients. All recipes include champagne, but disagree about the spirits included.

SERVES 1

4–6 cracked ice cubes, 2 measures brandy, 1 measure lemon juice,

1 tbsp sugar syrup (see page 9), chilled champagne, to top off,

twist of lemon peel, to decorate

1 Put the cracked ice cubes into a cocktail shaker. Pour the brandy, lemon juice, and sugar syrup over the ice and shake vigorously until a frost forms.

2 Strain into a chilled highball glass and top off with champagne. Decorate the glass with the lemon twist.

VIVE LA FRANCE

FRENCH 75 (second version): put 4–6 cracked ice cubes into a cocktail shaker. Pour 2 measures Plymouth gin and 1 measure lime juice over the ice and shake vigorously until a frost forms. Strain into a chilled wine glass and top off with chilled champagne. Decorate with a cocktail cherry.

FRENCH 75 (third version): put 1 teaspoon superfine sugar into a tall, chilled glass. Add 1 measure lemon juice and stir until the sugar has dissolved. Fill the glass with cracked ice cubes. Pour 2 measures gin over the ice and top off with chilled champagne. Decorate with slices of orange and cocktail cherries.

LONDON FRENCH 75: make the second version of a French 75, but substitute London gin for the Plymouth gin and lemon juice for the lime.

FRENCH ROSE: put 4–6 ice cubes into a mixing glass. Pour 2 measures gin, 1 measure cherry brandy, and 1 measure dry vermouth over the ice. Stir well and strain into a chilled cocktail glass.

b and b

Although elaborate concoctions are great fun to mix—and drink—some of the best cocktails are the simplest. B and B—brandy and Bénédictine—couldn't be easier, but it has a superbly subtle flavor.

SERVES 1

4–6 cracked ice cubes, 1 measure brandy, 1 measure Bénédictine

1 Put the ice cubes into a mixing glass. Pour the brandy and Bénédictine over the ice and stir to mix.

2 Strain into a chilled cocktail glass.

VARIATIONS

BIG BOY: put 4–6 cracked ice cubes into a mixing glass. Pour 2 measures brandy, 1 measure triple sec, and 1 measure lemon juice over the ice. Stir to mix, then strain into a chilled cocktail glass.

BOOSTER: put 4–6 cracked ice cubes into a cocktail shaker. Pour 2 measures brandy and 1 teaspoon clear Curaçao over the ice and add 1 egg white. Shake until a frost forms. Strain into a chilled cocktail glass.

FRENCH CONNECTION: put 4–6 cracked ice cubes into a small, chilled glass. Pour 2 measures brandy and 1 measure amaretto over the ice. Stir well to mix. Half fill a small, chilled glass with cracked ice cubes and strain the cocktail over them.

LUGGER: put 4–6 cracked ice cubes into a cocktail shaker. Pour 2 measures brandy, 1½ measures apple brandy, and ¼ teaspoon apricot brandy over the ice. Shake vigorously until a frost forms, then strain into a chilled cocktail glass.

HELL: put 4–6 cracked ice cubes into a mixing glass and add 1 measure brandy and 1 measure crème de menthe. Stir well to mix, then strain into a chilled cocktail glass. Sprinkle with a pinch of cayenne pepper.

corpse reviver

This cocktail is not designed to deal with a hangover the morning after, but is a great pick-me-up after a busy day to get you in the mood to party. Note that it will not prevent your needing a different kind of corpse reviver or some other sort of pick-me-up (see below) next day. None of these cocktails comes with a medical guarantee.

SERVES 1

4–6 cracked ice cubes, 2 measures brandy,

1 measure apple brandy, 1 measure sweet vermouth

1 Put the cracked ice into a mixing glass. Pour the brandy, apple brandy, and vermouth over the ice. Stir gently to mix.

2 Strain into a chilled cocktail glass.

OTHER DESPERATE MEASURES

STOMACH REVIVER: put 4–6 cracked ice cubes into a glass. Dash Angostura bitters over the ice and pour in 2 measures brandy, and 1 measure Fernet Branca. Stir well, then strain into a chilled cocktail glass.

PRAIRIE OYSTER: put 4–6 cracked ice cubes into a cocktail shaker. Dash Tabasco sauce over the ice and pour in 2 measures brandy, ½ measure Worcestershire sauce, ½ measure red wine vinegar, and 1 teaspoon tomato catsup. Shake until a frost forms. Strain into a chilled glass, float an unbroken egg yolk on top, and sprinkle with cayenne pepper. Swallow the cocktail in one without breaking the egg yolk. (For an Open Prairie Oyster see page 79.)

BARTENDER'S TIP

Grenadine is a sweet, pink-colored syrup made from pomegranates and can be used to sweeten and color both alcoholic and nonalcoholic cocktails. It has a distinctive, but not strong, flavor, and if you don't like it, you can substitute sugar syrup (see page 9). Grenadine is also very sweet, so you may wish to add less if you find it too sweet.

between the sheets

Since the name of this cocktail always seems to imply romance and hints that the sheets in question are, at the very least, satin, make it for two people. Certainly, this delicious concoction is as smooth as silk.

SERVES 2

8–10 cracked ice cubes, 4 measures brandy, 3 measures white rum,

1 measure clear Curaçao, 1 measure lemon juice

1 Put the cracked ice into a cocktail shaker. Pour the brandy, rum, Curaçao, and lemon juice over the ice. Shake vigorously until a frost forms.

2 Strain into two chilled wine glasses or goblets.

MORE ROMANTIC MOMENTS

These variations all serve one person.

BETWEEN SHEETS: put 4–6 cracked ice cubes into a cocktail shaker. Pour 1 measure brandy, 1 measure white rum, 1 measure triple sec, and 1 measure lemon juice over the ice. Shake vigorously until a frost forms, then strain into a chilled shot glass.

GRAND PASSION: put 4–6 cracked ice cubes into a cocktail shaker and add 2 measures gin, 1 measure dry vermouth, 1 measure passion fruit syrup, and ½ measure lemon juice. Shake until a frost forms. Strain into a chilled cocktail glass and decorate with an orange peel twist.

NIGHT OF PASSION: put 4–6 cracked ice cubes into a cocktail shaker. Pour 2 measures gin, 1 measure triple sec, 2 measures peach juice, 2 measures passion fruit juice, and 1 tablespoon lemon juice over the ice. Shake vigorously until a frost forms, then strain into a chilled glass.

BEDTIME BOUNCER: put 4–6 cracked ice cubes into a cocktail shaker. Pour 2 measures brandy and 1 measure triple sec over the ice. Shake vigorously until a frost forms and strain into a chilled glass. Top off with bitter lemon and decorate with an orange peel twist.

mint julep

A julep is simply a mixed drink sweetened with syrup—but the mere word conjures up images of ante-bellum cotton plantations and a long-gone, leisurely, and gracious way of life.

SERVES 1

leaves of 1 fresh mint sprig, 1 tbsp sugar syrup (see page 9),

6–8 crushed ice cubes, 3 measures bourbon whiskey,

fresh mint sprig, to decorate

1 Put the mint leaves and sugar syrup into a small, chilled glass and mash with a teaspoon. Add the crushed ice to fill the glass, then add the bourbon.

2 Decorate with the mint sprig.

VARIATIONS

FROZEN MINT JULEP: put 4–6 crushed ice cubes into a blender or food processor. Add 2 measures bourbon whiskey, 1 measure lemon juice, 1 measure sugar syrup (see page 9), and 6 fresh mint leaves. Process at low speed until slushy. Pour into a small, chilled glass and decorate with a fresh mint sprig.

BRANDY JULEP: fill a chilled glass with cracked ice. Add 2 measures brandy, 1 teaspoon sugar syrup (see page 9), and 4 fresh mint leaves. Stir well to mix and decorate with a fresh mint sprig and a slice of lemon. Serve with a straw.

JOCOSE JULEP: put 4–6 crushed ice cubes into a blender. Pour in 3 measures bourbon whiskey, 1 measure green crème de menthe, 1½ measures lime juice, and 1 teaspoon sugar syrup (see page 9). Add 5 fresh mint leaves. Process until smooth. Fill a chilled glass with cracked ice cubes and pour in the cocktail. Top off with sparkling mineral water and stir gently. Decorate with a fresh mint sprig.

whiskey sour

Sours are short drinks, flavored with lemon or lime juice. They can be made with almost any spirit, although Whiskey Sour was the original and, for many, is still the favorite.

SERVES 1

4–6 cracked ice cubes, 2 measures American blended whiskey,

1 measure lemon juice, 1 tsp sugar syrup (see page 9),

cocktail cherry, slice of orange, to decorate

1 Put the cracked ice into a cocktail shaker. Pour the whiskey, lemon juice, and sugar syrup over the ice. Shake vigorously until a frost forms.

2 Strain into a chilled cocktail glass and decorate with the cherry and orange slice.

VARIATIONS

BOURBON SOUR: substitute bourbon for the blended whiskey and decorate with an orange slice.

BRANDY SOUR: substitute 2½ measures brandy for the blended whiskey.

POLYNESIAN SOUR: put 4–6 cracked ice cubes into a cocktail shaker and add 2 measures white rum, ½ measure lemon juice, ½ measure orange juice, and ½ measure guava juice. Shake until a frost forms, then pour into a chilled cocktail glass. Decorate the glass with a slice of orange.

FIREMAN'S SOUR: put 4–6 cracked ice cubes into a cocktail shaker and add 2 measures white rum, 1½ measures lime juice, 1 tablespoon grenadine, and 1 teaspoon sugar syrup (see page 9). Shake until a frost forms. Strain into a cocktail glass and decorate with a cocktail cherry and a slice of lemon.

STREGA SOUR: put 4–6 cracked ice cubes into a cocktail shaker. Pour 2 measures gin, 1 measure Strega, and 1 measure lemon juice over the ice. Shake vigorously until a frost forms. Strain into a cocktail glass and decorate with a slice of lemon.

manhattan

Said to have been invented by Sir Winston Churchill's American mother, Jennie, the Manhattan is one of many cocktails named after places in New York City. The center of sophistication in the Jazz Age, the city is, once again, buzzing with cocktail bars for a new generation.

SERVES 1

4–6 cracked ice cubes, dash of Angostura bitters, 3 measures rye whiskey, 1 measure sweet vermouth, cocktail cherry, to decorate

1 Put the cracked ice into a mixing glass. Dash the Angostura bitters over the ice and pour in the whiskey and vermouth. Stir well to mix.

2 Strain into a chilled glass and decorate with the cherry.

CITY LIGHTS

HARLEM COCKTAIL: put 4–6 cracked ice cubes into a cocktail shaker. Pour 2 measures gin, 1½ measures pineapple juice, and 1 teaspoon Maraschino over the ice, and add 1 tablespoon chopped fresh pineapple. Shake vigorously until a frost forms, then strain into a small, chilled glass.

BROOKLYN: put 4–6 cracked ice cubes into a mixing glass. Dash Amer Picon and Maraschino over the ice and pour in 2 measures rye whiskey and 1 measure dry vermouth. Stir to mix, then strain into a chilled cocktail glass.

FIFTH AVENUE: pour 1½ measures chilled dark crème de cacao into a small, chilled, straight-sided glass. With a steady hand, pour 1½ measures chilled apricot brandy on top, without mixing, then carefully pour 3/4 measure chilled light cream on top, again without mixing.

CONEY ISLAND BABY: put 4–6 cracked ice cubes into a cocktail shaker. Pour 2 measures peppermint schnapps and 1 measure dark crème de cacao over the ice. Shake vigorously until a frost forms. Fill a small, chilled glass with cracked ice and strain the cocktail over it. Top off with club soda and stir gently.

white lady

Simple, elegant, subtle, and much more powerful than appearance suggests, this is the perfect cocktail to serve before an al fresco summer dinner.

SERVES 1

4–6 cracked ice cubes, 2 measures gin,

1 measure triple sec, 1 measure lemon juice

1 Put the ice into a cocktail shaker. Pour the gin, triple sec, and lemon juice over the ice. Shake vigorously until a frost forms.

2 Strain into a chilled cocktail glass.

VARIATIONS

GREEN LADY: put 4–6 cracked ice cubes into a cocktail shaker. Dash lime juice over the ice and pour in 2 measures gin and 1 measure green Chartreuse. Shake vigorously until a frost forms, then strain into a chilled cocktail glass.

APRICOT LADY: put 4–6 cracked ice cubes into a cocktail shaker. Pour 1½ measures white rum, 1 measure apricot brandy, 1 tablespoon lime juice, and ½ teaspoon triple sec over the ice, and add 1 egg white. Shake vigorously until a frost forms. Half fill a small, chilled glass with cracked ice. Strain the cocktail over the ice and decorate with a slice of orange.

BLUE LADY: put 4–6 cracked ice cubes into a cocktail shaker. Pour 2½ measures blue Curaçao, 1 measure white crème de cacao, and 1 measure light cream over the ice. Shake until a frost forms, then strain into a chilled cocktail glass.

MY FAIR LADY: put 4–6 cracked ice cubes into a cocktail shaker. Dash strawberry liqueur over the ice, pour in 2 measures gin, 1 measure orange juice, 1 measure lemon juice, and add 1 egg white. Shake vigorously until a frost forms. Strain into a chilled cocktail glass.

SHADY LADY: put 4–6 cracked ice cubes into a cocktail shaker. Dash lime juice over the ice and pour in 3 measures tequila, 1 measure apple brandy, and 1 measure cranberry juice. Shake until a frost forms. Strain into a chilled cocktail glass.

alexander

This creamy, chocolate-flavored, gin-based cocktail, decorated with grated nutmeg, is the head of an extended family of cocktails, which continues to grow.

SERVES 1

4–6 cracked ice cubes, 1 measure gin, 1 measure crème de cacao, 1 measure light cream, freshly grated nutmeg, to decorate

1 Put the cracked ice cubes into a cocktail shaker. Pour the gin, crème de cacao, and light cream over the ice. Shake vigorously until a frost forms.

2 Strain into a chilled cocktail glass and sprinkle with the nutmeg.

FAMILY CONNECTIONS

ALEXANDER'S SISTER: put 4–6 cracked ice cubes into a cocktail shaker. Pour 2 measures gin, 1 measure green crème de menthe, and 1 measure light cream over the ice. Shake until a frost forms, then strain into a chilled cocktail glass and decorate with freshly grated nutmeg.

ALEXANDER'S SISTER-IN-LAW: put 4–6 cracked ice cubes into a cocktail shaker. Pour 1 measure gin, 1 measure white crème de menthe, and 1 measure light cream over the ice. Shake until a frost forms, strain into a chilled cocktail glass, and decorate with freshly grated nutmeg.

ALEXANDER BABY: put 4–6 cracked ice cubes into a cocktail shaker. Pour 2 measures white rum, 1 measure crème de cacao, and ½ measure light cream over the ice. Shake until a frost forms, then strain into a chilled cocktail glass, and decorate with freshly grated nutmeg.

BRANDY ALEXANDER: put 4–6 cracked ice cubes into a cocktail shaker. Pour 1½ measures brandy, 1½ measures dark crème de cacao, and 1½ measures light cream over the ice. Shake vigorously until a frost forms, then strain into a chilled cocktail glass.

BARTENDER'S TIP

For Alexander's Daughter, a nonalcoholic version, see page 93.

tom collins

This cocktail combines gin, lemon juice, and club soda to make a cooling long drink. This is a venerable cocktail, but the progenitor of several generations of the Collins family of drinks, scattered across the globe, was the popular John Collins cocktail.

SERVES 1

5–6 cracked ice cubes, 3 measures gin, 2 measures lemon juice,

½ measure sugar syrup (see page 9), club soda, to top off,

slice of lemon, to decorate

1 Put the cracked ice into a cocktail shaker. Pour the gin, lemon juice, and sugar syrup over the ice. Shake vigorously until a frost forms.

2 Strain into a tall, chilled glass and top off with club soda. Decorate with a slice of lemon.

VARIATIONS

JOHN COLLINS: substitute Dutch gin or genever for the dry gin.

MICK COLLINS: substitute Irish whiskey for the gin.

PIERRE COLLINS: substitute brandy for the gin.

PEDRO COLLINS: substitute white rum for the gin.

COLONEL COLLINS: substitute bourbon for the gin.

MAC COLLINS: substitute Scotch whisky for the gin.

JUAN COLLINS: half fill a chilled glass with cracked ice cubes and pour in 2 measures white tequila, 1 measure lemon juice, and 1 teaspoon sugar syrup (see page 9). Top off with sparkling water and stir gently. Decorate with a cocktail cherry.

COUNTRY COUSIN COLLINS: put 4–6 crushed ice cubes into a blender. Dash orange bitters over the ice. Add 2 measures apple brandy, 1 measure lemon juice, and ½ teaspoon sugar syrup (see page 9). Blend at medium speed for 10 seconds. Pour into a tall, chilled glass. Top off with sparkling water. Stir and decorate with a lemon slice.

orange blossom

It is disappointing to discover that the pretty name of this cocktail is derived from the practice of adding fresh orange juice to bathtub gin during the years of Prohibition in order to conceal its filthy flavor. Made with good-quality gin, which needs no such concealment, it is delightfully refreshing.

SERVES 1

4–6 cracked ice cubes, 2 measures gin, 2 measures orange juice, slice of orange, to decorate

1 Put the cracked ice cubes into a cocktail shaker. Pour the gin and orange juice over the ice and shake vigorously until a frost forms.

2 Strain into a chilled cocktail glass and decorate with the orange slice.

VARIATIONS

HAWAIIAN ORANGE BLOSSOM: put 4–6 cracked ice cubes into a cocktail shaker. Pour 2 measures gin, 1 measure triple sec, 2 measures orange juice, and 1 measure pineapple juice over the ice. Shake vigorously until a frost forms, then strain into a chilled wine glass.

KENTUCKY ORANGE BLOSSOM: put 4–6 cracked ice cubes into a cocktail shaker. Pour 2 measures bourbon, 1 measure orange juice, and ½ measure triple sec over the ice. Shake vigorously until a frost forms. Strain into a chilled cocktail glass and decorate with an orange slice.

MAGNOLIA BLOSSOM: put 4–6 cracked ice cubes into a cocktail shaker. Pour 2 measures gin, 1 measure lemon juice, and 1 measure light cream over the ice. Shake vigorously until a frost forms. Strain into a chilled cocktail glass.

APPLE BLOSSOM: put 4–6 cracked ice cubes into a mixing glass. Pour 2 measures brandy, 1½ measures apple juice, and ½ teaspoon lemon juice over the ice, and stir well to mix. Half fill a small, chilled glass with ice and strain the cocktail over it. Decorate with a slice of lemon.

CHERRY BLOSSOM: put 4–6 cracked ice cubes into a cocktail shaker. Dash clear Curaçao, grenadine, and lemon juice over the ice, and pour in 2 measures brandy and 2 measures cherry brandy. Shake vigorously until a frost forms, then strain into a chilled cocktail glass.

old fashioned

So ubiquitous is this cocktail that a small, straight-sided glass is known as an Old Fashioned glass. It is a perfect illustration of the saying, "Sometimes the old ones are the best."

SERVES 1

sugar cube, dash of Angostura bitters, 1 tsp water,

2 measures bourbon or rye whiskey, 4–6 cracked ice cubes

lemon peel twist, to decorate

1 Place the sugar cube in a small, chilled Old Fashioned glass. Dash the bitters over the cube and add the water. Mash with a spoon until the sugar has dissolved.

2 Pour the bourbon or rye whiskey into the glass and stir. Add the cracked ice cubes and decorate with the lemon peel twist.

"NOT OLD, BUT MELLOW"

OLD ETONIAN: put 4–6 cracked ice cubes into a mixing glass. Dash crème de noyaux and orange bitters over the ice and pour in 1 measure gin and 1 measure Lillet. Stir, then strain into a chilled cocktail glass. Squeeze over a piece of orange peel.

OLD PAL: put 4–6 cracked ice cubes into a cocktail shaker. Pour 2 measures rye whiskey, 1½ measures Campari, and 1 measure sweet vermouth over the ice. Shake vigorously until a frost forms, then strain into a chilled cocktail glass.

OLD TROUT: put 4–6 cracked ice cubes into a cocktail shaker. Pour 1 measure Campari and 2 measures orange juice over the ice. Shake vigorously until a frost forms. Fill a tall glass with ice cubes and strain the cocktail over them. Top off with sparkling mineral water and decorate with a slice of orange.

OLD PALE: put 4–6 cracked ice cubes into a mixing glass. Pour 2 measures bourbon, 1 measure Campari, and 1 measure dry vermouth over the ice. Stir well, then strain into a chilled cocktail glass. Squeeze over a piece of lemon peel.

Cocktails and Punches

martini

For many, this is the ultimate cocktail. It is named after its inventor, Martini de Anna de Toggia, and not the famous brand of vermouth. The original version comprised equal measures of gin and vermouth, now known as a Fifty-Fifty, but the proportions vary, up to the Ultra Dry Martini, when the glass is merely rinsed out with vermouth before the gin is poured in.

SERVES 1

4–6 cracked ice cubes, 3 measures gin,

1 tsp dry vermouth, or to taste, cocktail olive, to decorate

1 Put the cracked ice cubes into a mixing glass. Pour the gin and vermouth over the ice and stir well to mix.

2 Strain into a chilled cocktail glass and decorate with a cocktail olive.

VARIATIONS

GIBSON: decorate with 2–3 cocktail onions, instead of an olive.

VODKA MARTINI: substitute vodka for the gin.

TEQUINI: put 4–6 cracked ice cubes into a mixing glass. Dash Angostura bitters over the ice and pour in 3 measures white tequila and ½ measure dry vermouth. Stir well to mix, strain into a chilled cocktail glass and decorate with a twist of lemon.

DIRTY MARTINI: put 4–6 cracked ice cubes into a cocktail shaker. Pour 3 measures gin, 1 measure dry vermouth, and ½ measure brine from a jar of cocktail olives over the ice. Shake vigorously until a frost forms. Strain into a chilled cocktail glass and decorate with a cocktail olive.

DID YOU KNOW?

Not only did James Bond always demand that his Martini should be shaken, not stirred, but his creator, Ian Fleming, also followed this practice.

singapore sling

In the days of the British Empire, the privileged would gather in the relative cool of the evening to refresh parched throats and gossip about the day's events at exclusive clubs. Those days are long gone, but a Singapore Sling is still the ideal thirst-quencher on hot evenings.

SERVES 1

10–12 cracked ice cubes, 2 measures gin, 1 measure cherry brandy,

1 measure lemon juice, 1 tsp grenadine, club soda, to top off,

lime peel, cocktail cherries, to decorate

1 Put 4–6 cracked ice cubes into a cocktail shaker. Pour the gin, cherry brandy, lemon juice, and grenadine over the ice. Shake vigorously until a frost forms.

2 Half fill a chilled highball glass with cracked ice cubes and strain the cocktail over them. Top off with club soda and then decorate with a twist of lime peel and cocktail cherries.

VARIATIONS

SWEET SINGAPORE SLING: put 4–6 cracked ice cubes into a cocktail shaker. Dash lemon juice over the ice and pour in 1 measure gin and 2 measures cherry brandy. Shake vigorously until a frost forms. Half fill a chilled glass with cracked ice cubes and strain the cocktail over them. Top off with club soda and decorate with cocktail cherries.

GIN SLING: put 1 teaspoon sugar in a mixing glass. Add 1 measure lemon juice and 1 teaspoon water and stir until the sugar has dissolved. Pour in 2 measures gin and stir to mix. Half fill a small, chilled glass with ice and strain the cocktail over it. Decorate with an orange peel twist.

WHISKEY SLING: put 1 teaspoon sugar in a mixing glass. Add 1 measure lemon juice and 1 teaspoon water and stir until the sugar has dissolved. Pour in 2 measures American blended whiskey and stir to mix. Half fill a small, chilled glass with ice and strain the cocktail over it. Decorate with an orange peel twist.

Cocktails and Punches

maiden's blush

The name of this cocktail aptly describes its pretty color. Too many, however, and maidenly modesty may be abandoned and blushing could become compulsory.

SERVES 1

4–6 cracked ice cubes, 2 measures gin,

½ tsp triple sec, ½ tsp grenadine, ½ tsp lemon juice

1 Put the cracked ice cubes into a cocktail shaker. Pour the gin, triple sec, grenadine, and lemon juice over the ice. Shake vigorously until a frost forms.

2 Strain into a chilled cocktail glass or small highball glass.

MARITAL STATUS

MAIDENLY BLUSH: put 4–6 cracked ice cubes into a mixing glass. Pour 2 measures gin and 1 measure Pernod over the ice. Stir well to mix, then strain into a chilled cocktail glass.

MAIDEN'S PRAYER: put 4–6 cracked ice cubes into a cocktail shaker. Pour 1 measure gin, 1 measure triple sec, 1 teaspoon orange juice, and 1 teaspoon lemon juice over the ice. Shake vigorously until a frost forms, then strain into a chilled cocktail glass.

VIRGIN'S PRAYER: put 4–6 cracked ice cubes into a cocktail shaker. Pour 1 measure white rum, 1 measure dark rum, 1 measure Kahlúa, 1 teaspoon lemon juice, and 2 teaspoons orange juice over the ice. Shake vigorously until a frost forms, then strain into a small, chilled glass. Decorate with slices of lime.

WEDDING BELLE: put 4–6 cracked ice cubes into a cocktail shaker. Pour 2 measures gin, 2 measures Dubonnet, 1 measure cherry brandy, and 1 measure orange juice over the ice. Shake until a frost forms, then strain into a cocktail glass.

WIDOW'S WISH: put 4–6 cracked ice cubes into a mixing glass. Pour 2 measures Bénédictine over the ice and add 1 egg. Shake vigorously until a frost forms, then strain into a chilled glass. Top off with light cream.

piña colada

One of the younger generation of classics, this became popular during the cocktail revival of the 1980s and has remained so ever since.

SERVES 1

4–6 crushed ice cubes, 2 measures white rum, 1 measure dark rum,

3 measures pineapple juice, 2 measures coconut cream,

pineapple wedges, to decorate

1 Put the crushed ice into a blender and add the white rum, dark rum, pineapple juice, and coconut cream. Blend until smooth.

2 Pour, without straining, into a tall, chilled glass and decorate with pineapple wedges speared on a cocktail stick.

VARIATIONS

LIGHTEN UP PIÑA COLADA: put 4–6 cracked ice cubes into a cocktail shaker. Pour 2 measures white rum, 2 measures Malibu, and 3 measures pineapple juice over the ice. Shake vigorously until a frost forms. Half fill a small, chilled glass with cracked ice cubes. Strain the cocktail over them. Decorate with a pineapple slice.

AMIGOS PIÑA COLADA (to serve 4): put 10–12 crushed ice cubes into a blender and add 1 cup white rum, 1¼ cups pineapple juice, 5 measures coconut cream, 2 measures dark rum, and 2 measures light cream. Blend until smooth. Pour, without straining, into long, chilled glasses and decorate with pineapple wedges speared on cocktail sticks.

STRAWBERRY COLADA: put 4–6 crushed ice cubes into a blender and add 3 measures golden rum, 4 measures pineapple juice, 1 measure coconut cream, and 6 hulled strawberries. Blend until smooth, then pour, without straining, into a tall, chilled glass. Decorate with pineapple wedges and strawberries speared on a cocktail stick.

daiquiri

Daiquiri is a town in Cuba, where this drink was said to have been invented in the early part of the twentieth century. A businessman had run out of imported gin, so he had to make do with the local drink—rum—which, at that time, was of unreliable quality. To ensure that his guests would find it palatable, he decided to mix it with other ingredients. This classic has since given rise to almost innumerable variations.

SERVES 1

4–6 cracked ice cubes, 2 measures white rum,

3/4 measure lime juice, 1/2 tsp sugar syrup (see page 9)

1 Put the cracked ice cubes into a cocktail shaker. Pour the rum, lime juice, and sugar syrup over the ice. Shake vigorously until a frost forms.

2 Strain into a chilled cocktail glass.

VARIATIONS

DERBY DAIQUIRI: put 4–6 crushed ice cubes into a blender and add 2 measures white rum, 1 measure orange juice, 1/2 measure triple sec, and 1/2 measure lime juice. Blend until smooth, then pour, without straining, into a chilled cocktail glass.

BANANA DAIQUIRI: put 4–6 crushed ice cubes into a blender and then add 2 measures white rum, 1/2 measure triple sec, 1/2 measure lime juice, 1/2 measure light cream, 1 teaspoon sugar syrup (see page 9), and 1/4 peeled and sliced banana. Blend until smooth, then pour the mixture, without straining, into a chilled goblet and decorate it with a slice of lime.

PASSIONATE DAIQUIRI: put 4–6 cracked ice cubes into a cocktail shaker. Pour 2 measures white rum, 1 measure lime juice, and 1/2 measure passion fruit syrup over the ice. Shake vigorously until a frost forms. Strain into a chilled cocktail glass and decorate with a cocktail cherry.

planter's punch

Derived from a Hindi word meaning five, punch is so called because, traditionally, it contained five ingredients. These should also include four basic flavors—strong, weak, sour, and sweet.

SERVES 1

10–12 cracked ice cubes, dash of grenadine, 2 measures white rum, 2 measures dark rum, 1 measure lemon juice, 1 measure lime juice, 1 tsp sugar syrup (see page 9), ¼ tsp triple sec, sparkling mineral water, to top off, slice of lemon, slice of lime, slice of pineapple, cocktail cherry, to decorate

1 Put 4–6 cracked ice cubes into a cocktail shaker. Dash the grenadine over the ice and pour in the white rum, dark rum, lemon juice, lime juice, sugar syrup, and triple sec. Shake vigorously until a frost forms.

2 Half fill a tall, chilled Collins glass with cracked ice cubes and strain the cocktail over them. Top off with sparkling mineral water and stir gently. Decorate with the lemon, lime, and pineapple slices, and a cherry.

VARIATIONS

PLANTATION PUNCH: put 4–6 cracked ice cubes into a cocktail shaker. Pour 2 measures dark rum, 1 measure Southern Comfort, and 1 measure lemon juice over the ice, and add 1 teaspoon brown sugar. Shake vigorously until a frost forms. Strain into a tall, chilled glass and top off, almost to the rim, with sparkling mineral water. Float 1 teaspoon of ruby port on top by pouring it gently over the back of a teaspoon and garnish with a lemon slice and an orange slice.

PLANTER'S COCKTAIL: put 4–6 cracked ice cubes into a cocktail shaker. Dash lemon juice over the ice and pour in 1 measure rum and 1 measure orange juice. Shake vigorously until a frost forms, then strain into a chilled cocktail glass.

Cocktails and Punches

margarita

The traditional way to drink tequila is to shake a little salt on the back of your hand between the thumb and forefinger and, holding a wedge of lime or lemon, lick the salt, suck the fruit, and then down a shot of tequila in one. This cocktail, attributed to Francisco Morales and invented in 1942 in Mexico, is a more civilized version.

SERVES 1

lime wedge, coarse salt, 4–6 cracked ice cubes, 3 measures white tequila,

1 measure triple sec, 2 measures lime juice, slice of lime, to decorate

1 Rub the rim of a chilled cocktail glass with the lime wedge and then dip in a saucer of coarse salt to frost.

2 Put the cracked ice cubes into a cocktail shaker. Pour the tequila, triple sec, and lime juice over the ice. Shake vigorously until a frost forms.

3 Strain into the prepared glass and decorate with the lime slice.

VARIATIONS

FROZEN MARGARITA: put 6–8 cracked ice cubes into a blender and add 2 measures white tequila, 1 measure lime juice, and ½ measure triple sec. Blend at low speed until slushy. Pour, without straining, into a chilled cocktail glass and decorate with a slice of lime.

BLUE MARGARITA: frost the rim of a chilled cocktail glass using a lime wedge and coarse salt (as above). Put 4–6 cracked ice cubes into a cocktail shaker. Pour 2 measures white tequila, 1 measure blue Curaçao, 1½ measures lime juice, and 1 tablespoon triple sec over the ice. Shake until a frost forms. Strain into the prepared glass. Decorate with a slice of lime.

5757 GIN MARGARITA (from the bar of the same name in the Four Seasons Hotel, New York City): put 4–6 cracked ice cubes into a cocktail shaker. Pour 1½ measures gin, ½ measure triple sec, and 1 measure lemon juice over the ice, and add sugar syrup (see page 9) to taste. Shake vigorously until a frost forms, then strain into a chilled cocktail glass.

tequila sunrise

This is one cocktail you shouldn't rush when making, otherwise you will spoil the attractive sunrise effect as the grenadine slowly spreads through the orange juice.

SERVES 1

4–6 cracked ice cubes, 2 parts white tequila, orange juice, to top off, 1 measure grenadine

1 Put the cracked ice cubes into a chilled highball glass. Pour the tequila over the ice and top off with the orange juice. Stir well to mix.

2 Slowly pour in the grenadine and serve with a straw.

VARIATIONS

BLINDING SUNRISE: put 4–6 cracked ice cubes into a cocktail shaker. Pour 1 measure white tequila, 1 measure vodka, 3 measures orange juice, and 1 teaspoon triple sec over the ice. Shake until a frost forms. Half fill a glass with cracked ice cubes and strain the cocktail over them. Slowly pour in 1 measure grenadine.

PACIFIC SUNRISE: put 4–6 cracked ice cubes into a cocktail shaker. Dash Angostura bitters over the ice and pour in 1 measure white tequila, 1 measure blue Curaçao, and 1 measure lime juice. Shake vigorously until a frost forms, then strain into a chilled cocktail glass.

DID YOU KNOW?

The popularity of tequila took producers by surprise. The agave plant from which it is made takes 8–10 years to mature: slow maturation and cultivation problems created a severe shortage by the year 2000, which resulted in rocketing prices and a lucrative trade in "cactus rustling."

bloody mary

This classic cocktail was invented in 1921 at the legendary Harry's Bar in Paris. There are numerous versions—some much hotter and spicier than others. Ingredients may include horseradish sauce in addition to or instead of Tabasco sauce, more or less tomato juice, and lime juice instead of lemon. Sometimes the glass is decorated with a sprig of mint. Whatever the version, all experts agree that it is essential to use the highest-quality ingredients.

SERVES 1

4–6 cracked ice cubes, dash of Worcestershire sauce, dash of Tabasco sauce,

2 measures vodka, 6 measures tomato juice, juice of ½ lemon,

pinch of celery salt, pinch of cayenne pepper,

celery stalk with leaves, slice of lemon, to decorate

1 Put the cracked ice into a cocktail shaker. Dash the Worcestershire sauce and Tabasco sauce over the ice and pour in the vodka, tomato juice, and lemon juice. Shake vigorously until a frost forms.

2 Strain into a chilled glass, add a pinch of celery salt and a pinch of cayenne, and decorate with a celery stalk and a slice of lemon.

VARIATIONS

BLOODY MARIA: substitute 2 measures white tequila for the vodka and add 1 teaspoon horseradish sauce, and a pinch of ground coriander. Decorate with a lime wedge.

COLD AND CLAMMY BLOODY MARY: substitute 3 measures clam juice for 3 of the measures of tomato juice and decorate with a scallion curl.

BULLSHOT: substitute 4 measures chilled beef bouillon for the tomato juice. Season with salt and freshly ground black pepper.

BARTENDER'S TIP

For a Bloody January and other non-alcoholic variations, see page 80.

black russian

History records only White and Red Russians. The omission of the Black Russian is a sad oversight. For a coffee liqueur, you can use either Tia Maria or Kahlúa, depending on your personal taste—the latter is sweeter.

SERVES 1

4–6 cracked ice cubes, 2 measures vodka, 1 measure coffee liqueur

1 Put the cracked ice cubes into a small, chilled highball glass. Pour the vodka and liqueur over the ice. Stir to mix.

THE RUSSIAN EMPIRE

TALL BLACK RUSSIAN: make a black Russian in a glass and top off with cola.

CREAM RUSSIAN: put 4–6 cracked ice cubes into a cocktail shaker. Pour 2 measures vodka, 1 measure coffee liqueur, and 1 measure light cream over the ice. Shake vigorously until a frost forms. Pour, without straining, into a small, chilled glass.

WHITE RUSSIAN: put 4–6 cracked ice cubes into a mixing glass. Pour 2 measures vodka and 1 measure white crème de menthe over the ice. Stir well and strain into a chilled cocktail glass.

RUSSIAN: put 4–6 cracked ice cubes into a mixing glass. Pour 1 measure vodka, 1 measure gin, and 1 measure white crème de cacao over the ice. Stir to mix thoroughly and strain into a chilled cocktail glass.

RUSSIAN BEAR: put 4–6 cracked ice cubes into a cocktail shaker. Pour 2 measures vodka, 1 measure dark crème de cacao, and ½ measure light cream over the ice. Shake vigorously until a frost forms. Strain into a chilled cocktail glass.

YELTSIN: put 4–6 cracked ice cubes into a mixing glass. Pour 2 measures vodka, 1 measure dry vermouth, and 1 measure medium sherry over the ice. Stir well and strain into a chilled cocktail glass. Squeeze lemon peel over.

screwdriver

Always use freshly squeezed orange juice to make this refreshing cocktail—it is just not the same with bottled juice. This simple, classic cocktail has given rise to numerous and increasingly elaborate variations.

SERVES 1

6–8 cracked ice cubes, 2 measures vodka,

orange juice, to top off, slice of orange, to decorate

1 Fill a chilled highball glass with cracked ice cubes. Pour the vodka over the ice and top off with orange juice.

2 Stir well to mix and decorate with a slice of orange.

VARIATIONS

CORDLESS SCREWDRIVER: pour 2 measures chilled vodka into a shot glass. Dip a wedge of orange into superfine sugar. Down the vodka in one go and suck the orange.

CREAMY SCREWDRIVER: put 4–6 crushed ice cubes into a blender. Add 2 measures vodka, 6 measures orange juice, 1 egg yolk, and ½ teaspoon sugar syrup (see page 9). Blend until smooth. Half fill a chilled glass with cracked ice cubes and pour the cocktail over them without straining.

HARVEY WALLBANGER: make a Screwdriver and then float 1 measure Galliano on top by pouring it gently over the back of a teaspoon.

BARTENDER'S TIP

Galliano is a honey- and vanilla-flavored liqueur from Italy. It is sold in tall, thin bottles, so bars store it on a top shelf up against the wall to avoid knocking it over.

DID YOU KNOW?

The Harvey Wallbanger is named after a California surfer who took such prodigious delight in drinking Screwdrivers topped with a Galliano float that he ricocheted from wall to wall on leaving the bar.

absinthe friend

A popular cocktail ingredient, the digestif absinthe is no longer available. Flavored with wormwood, which it is said reacts with alcohol to cause brain damage, absinthe was banned by law in 1915. However, various pastis, including Pernod and Ricard, are still available and make good substitutes.

SERVES 1

4–6 cracked ice cubes, dash of Angostura bitters, dash of sugar syrup (see page 9), 1 measure Pernod, 1 measure gin

1 Put the cracked ice cubes into a cocktail shaker. Dash the bitters and sugar syrup over the ice and pour in the Pernod and gin. Shake vigorously until a frost forms.

2 Strain into a chilled glass.

ABSINTHE MAKES THE HEART GROW FONDER

EARTHQUAKE: put 4–6 ice cubes into a mixing glass. Pour 1 measure Pernod, 1 measure gin, and 1 measure bourbon over the ice. Stir well to mix and strain into a chilled cocktail glass.

WALDORF: put 4–6 ice cubes into a cocktail shaker. Dash Angostura bitters over the ice and pour in 1 measure Pernod, 2 measures bourbon, and ½ measure sweet vermouth. Shake until a frost forms. Strain into a chilled cocktail glass.

YELLOW PARROT: put 4–6 ice cubes into a cocktail shaker. Pour 2 measures Pernod, 2 measures brandy, and 2 measures yellow Chartreuse over the ice. Shake vigorously until a frost forms. Strain into a chilled cocktail glass.

DID YOU KNOW?

When absinthe was first produced in the late eighteenth century, it was marketed as an aphrodisiac. It was also the favorite drink of Henri Toulouse-Lautrec, the great French artist.

Cocktails and Punches

negroni

This aristocratic cocktail was created by Count Negroni at the Bar Giacosa in Florence, although since then, the proportions of gin to Campari have altered.

SERVES 1

4–6 cracked ice cubes, 1 measure Campari, 1 measure gin,

½ measure sweet vermouth, twist of orange peel, to decorate

1 Put the cracked ice cubes into a mixing glass. Pour the Campari, gin, and vermouth over the ice. Stir well to mix.

2 Strain into a chilled glass and decorate with the orange twist.

THE FINE ITALIAN HAND

AMERICANO: put 4–6 ice cubes into a chilled glass. Pour 1½ measures sweet vermouth, and 1½ measures Campari over the ice. Top off with club soda and stir to mix thoroughly. Decorate with a twist of lemon peel.

ITALIAN STALLION: put 4–6 ice cubes into a mixing glass. Dash Angostura bitters over the ice and pour in 2 measures bourbon, 1 measure Campari, and ½ measure sweet vermouth. Stir well to mix, then strain into a chilled cocktail glass and decorate with a twist of lemon peel.

GENOA VODKA: put 4–6 ice cubes into a cocktail shaker. Pour 2 measures vodka, 1 measure Campari, and 3 measures orange juice over the ice. Shake vigorously until a frost forms. Strain into a chilled glass and decorate with a slice of orange.

ROSITA: put 4–6 ice cubes into a mixing glass. Pour 2 measures Campari, 2 measures white tequila, ½ measure dry vermouth, and ½ measure sweet vermouth over the ice. Stir well to mix, then strain into a small, chilled glass and decorate with a twist of lemon peel.

rolls royce

Hardly surprisingly, several classic cocktails have been named after this classic marque. This version was created by author H. E. Bates in his popular novel *The Darling Buds of May*.

SERVES 1

4–6 cracked ice cubes, dash of orange bitters, 2 measures dry vermouth, 1 measure dry gin, 1 measure Scotch whisky

1 Put the cracked ice cubes into a mixing glass. Dash the ice with the bitters.

2 Pour the vermouth, gin, and whisky over the ice and stir to mix. Strain into a chilled cocktail glass.

CLASSIC CARS

AMERICAN ROLLS ROYCE: put 4–6 ice cubes into a cocktail shaker. Pour 2 measures brandy, 1 measure triple sec, and 2 measures orange juice over the ice. Shake vigorously until a frost forms, then strain into a chilled cocktail glass.

BENTLEY: put 4–6 ice cubes into a mixing glass. Pour 2 measures Calvados and 1 measure red Dubonnet over the ice and stir. Strain the mixture into a chilled cocktail glass and decorate with a twist of lemon peel.

GOLDEN CADILLAC: put 4–6 ice cubes into a cocktail shaker. Pour 1 measure triple sec, 1 measure Galliano, and 1 measure light cream over the ice. Shake vigorously until a frost forms, then strain into a chilled cocktail glass.

DID YOU KNOW?

Writers and cocktails seem to have a special affinity. Raymond Chandler wrote affectionately of the Gimlet; Scott Fitzgerald evoked the glamor of cocktail society in **The Great Gatsby;** *and Ian Fleming created a variation of the Martini in* **Casino Royale.**

kir

As with the best mustard, crème de cassis production is centered on the French city of Dijon. This cocktail is named in commemoration of a partisan and mayor of the city, Félix Kir.

SERVES 1

4–6 cracked ice cubes, 2 measures crème de cassis,

white wine, to top off, twist of lemon peel, to decorate

1 Put the crushed ice cubes into a chilled wine glass. Pour the crème de cassis over the ice.

2 Top off with chilled white wine and stir well. Decorate with the lemon twist.

WINE TOPPERS

KIR ROYALE: substitute champagne for the white wine.

OSBORNE (named after Queen Victoria's Isle of Wight residence and apparently a favorite tipple of Her Majesty's): pour 3 measures claret and 1 measure Scotch whisky into a goblet and stir to mix.

BELLINI (created at Harry's Bar, Venice, and named after the Renaissance artist): fill a goblet with crushed ice and dash over grenadine. Pour in 1 measure peach juice, then top off with chilled champagne. Decorate with a peeled, fresh peach slice.

BELLINITINI: put 4–6 cracked ice cubes into a cocktail shaker. Pour in 2 measures vodka, 1 measure peach schnapps, and 1 measure peach juice. Shake until a frost forms, then strain into a chilled goblet. Top off with chilled champagne.

RIKKI-TIKKI-TAVI: put a sugar cube into a chilled champagne flute and dash with Angostura bitters until red but still intact. Pour in 1 teaspoon brandy and 1 teaspoon clear Curaçao and top off with chilled champagne.

BARTENDER'S TIP

For a nonalcoholic Faux Kir and variations, see page 84. For a nonalcoholic Baby Bellini, see page 85.

sherry cobbler

A long drink made with syrup and fresh fruit garnishes, Sherry Cobbler is the original, but there are now numerous and often more potent variations.

SERVES 1

6–8 cracked ice cubes, ¼ tsp sugar syrup (see page 9),

¼ tsp clear Curaçao, 4 measures Amontillado sherry,

pineapple wedges, twist of lemon peel, to decorate

1 Fill a wine glass with crushed ice. Add the sugar syrup and Curaçao and stir until a frost forms.

2 Pour in the sherry and stir well. Decorate with pineapple wedges speared on a cocktail stick and the lemon twist.

VARIATIONS

CHAMPAGNE COBBLER: put 4–6 cracked ice cubes into a goblet. Pour 1 measure brandy and 1 measure clear Curaçao over the ice and top off with chilled champagne. Decorate with a slice of orange.

BOURBON COBBLER: put 1 teaspoon superfine sugar into a tall, chilled glass and dash lemon juice over it. Add 6 cracked ice cubes and pour in 2 measures bourbon and 2 measures Southern Comfort. Top off with club soda and stir to mix. Decorate with a peach slice.

BRANDY COBBLER: put 1 teaspoon superfine sugar into a small, chilled glass and add 3 measures sparkling mineral water. Stir until the sugar has dissolved, then fill the glass with cracked ice. Pour in 2 measures brandy and stir well. Decorate with a slice of lemon and a cocktail cherry.

RUM COBBLER: put 1 teaspoon superfine sugar into a chilled goblet. Add 2 measures sparkling mineral water and stir until the sugar has dissolved. Fill the glass with cracked ice and pour in 2 measures white rum. Stir well and decorate with a lime slice and an orange slice.

buck's fizz

Invented at Buck's Club in London, the original was invariably made with Bollinger champagne and it is true that the better the quality of the champagne, the better the flavor.

SERVES 1

2 measures chilled champagne, 2 measures chilled orange juice

1 Pour the champagne into a chilled champagne flute, then pour in the orange juice.

VARIATIONS

DUCK'S FIZZ: substitute Canard-Duchêne champagne for the Bollinger.

MIMOSA: pour the orange juice into the flute and then the champagne. Stir gently. You can use sparkling white wine instead of champagne.

BLACK VELVET: pour 1¼ cups chilled champagne or sparkling wine and 1¼ cups chilled stout into a chilled glass at the same time. Do not stir.

SOYER AU CHAMPAGNE: put 1 scoop vanilla ice cream into a wine glass and add ¼ teaspoon brandy, ¼ teaspoon triple sec, and ¼ teaspoon Maraschino. Stir to mix, then top off with chilled champagne. Stir gently and decorate with a cocktail cherry.

CHAMPAGNE CUP: pour ½ measure brandy and ½ measure clear Curaçao into a chilled wine glass. Add 1 ice cube and top off with champagne. Decorate with a sprig of fresh mint and a slice of orange.

SPRITZER: fill a wine glass with cracked ice cubes and pour in 3 measures white wine. Top off with club soda or sparkling mineral water and decorate with a twist of lemon peel.

sidecar

Cointreau is the best-known brand of the orange-flavored liqueur known generically as triple sec. It is drier and stronger than Curaçao and is always colorless.

SERVES 1

4–6 cracked ice cubes, 2 measures brandy, 1 measure triple sec,

1 measure lemon juice, orange peel twist, to decorate

1 Put the ice into a cocktail shaker. Pour the brandy, triple sec, and lemon juice over the ice and shake vigorously until a frost forms.

2 Strain into a chilled glass and decorate with the orange peel twist.

VARIATIONS

CHAMPAGNE SIDECAR: make a Sidecar as above, but strain it into a chilled champagne flute, and then top off with chilled champagne.

CHELSEA SIDECAR: put 4–6 cracked ice cubes into a cocktail shaker. Pour 2 measures gin, 1 measure triple sec, and 1 measure lemon juice over the ice. Shake vigorously until a frost forms, then strain into a chilled cocktail glass. Decorate with a lemon peel twist.

BOSTON SIDECAR: put 4–6 cracked ice cubes into a cocktail shaker. Pour 1½ measures white rum, ½ measure brandy, ½ measure triple sec, and ½ measure lemon juice over the ice and shake vigorously until a frost forms. Strain into a chilled cocktail glass and decorate with an orange peel twist.

POLISH SIDECAR: put 4–6 cracked ice cubes into a cocktail shaker. Pour 2 measures gin, 1 measure blackberry brandy, and 1 measure lemon juice over the ice. Shake until a frost forms, then strain into a chilled cocktail glass. Decorate with a fresh blackberry.

bronx

Like Manhattan, the New York borough of the Bronx—and also the river of the same name—have been immortalized in cocktail bars throughout the world.

SERVES 1

4–6 cracked ice cubes, 2 measures gin, 1 measure orange juice,

½ measure dry vermouth, ½ measure sweet vermouth

1 Put the cracked ice cubes into a mixing glass. Pour the gin, orange juice, and dry and sweet vermouth over the ice. Stir to mix.

2 Strain into a chilled cocktail glass.

VARIATIONS

BRONX RIVER: put 4–6 cracked ice cubes into a cocktail shaker. Pour 2 measures gin, 1 measure sweet vermouth, 1 measure lemon juice, and ½ teaspoon sugar syrup (see page 9) over the ice. Shake vigorously until a frost forms. Strain into a chilled cocktail glass.

BRONX SILVER: put 4–6 cracked ice cubes into a cocktail shaker. Pour 2 measures gin, 1 measure orange juice, ½ measure dry vermouth, and 1 egg white over the ice. Shake vigorously until a frost forms, then strain into a chilled cocktail glass.

BRONX CHEER: almost fill a tall glass with cracked ice cubes. Pour 2 measures apricot brandy over the ice and top off with raspberry soda. Stir gently, decorate with orange peel and a fresh raspberry, and serve with a straw.

BRONX EMPRESS: put 4–6 cracked ice cubes into a cocktail shaker. Dash Pernod over the ice and pour in 1 measure gin, 1 measure orange juice, and 1 measure dry vermouth. Shake vigorously until a frost forms. Strain into a chilled cocktail glass.

BRONX TERRACE: put 4–6 cracked ice cubes into a cocktail shaker. Pour 2 measures gin, 1 measure lime juice, and ½ measure dry vermouth over the ice. Shake vigorously until a frost forms. Strain into a chilled cocktail glass and decorate with a cocktail cherry.

Contemporary Cocktails

highland fling

Blended whisky is best suited to cocktails—single malts should always be drunk neat or simply with a little added mineral water. However, a throat-burning, harsh blend will make a mixture closer to rocket fuel than a cocktail and no amount of additional flavors will improve it.

SERVES 1

4–6 cracked ice cubes, dash of Angostura bitters, 2 measures Scotch whisky, 1 measure sweet vermouth, cocktail olive, to decorate

1 Put the cracked ice into a mixing glass. Dash Angostura bitters over the ice. Pour the whisky and vermouth over the ice.

2 Stir well to mix and strain into a chilled glass. Decorate with a cocktail olive.

VARIATIONS

AFFINITY: put 4–6 cracked ice cubes into a mixing glass. Dash Angostura bitters over the ice and pour in 1 measure Scotch whisky, 1 measure dry vermouth, and 1 measure sweet vermouth. Stir well to mix, then pour into a chilled cocktail glass.

THISTLE: put 4–6 cracked ice cubes into a mixing glass. Dash Angostura bitters over the ice and pour in 2 measures Scotch whisky and 1½ measures sweet vermouth. Stir and strain into a chilled cocktail glass.

FLYING SCOTSMAN: put 4–6 crushed ice cubes into a blender, dash Angostura bitters over the ice, and add 2 measures Scotch whisky, 1 measure sweet vermouth, and ¼ teaspoon sugar syrup (see page 9). Blend until slushy and pour into a small, chilled glass.

DID YOU KNOW?

Angostura bitters were created by a German surgeon as a result of his work with herbal medicines in South America. His descendants still keep the secret of his formula.

panda

Slivovitz is a colorless plum brandy, usually made from Mirabelle and Switzen plums. It is usually drunk straight, but can add a fruity note to cocktails. If it is not available, you could substitute apricot, peach, or cherry brandy—all fruits from the same family—but the cocktail will not look or taste quite the same.

SERVES 1

4–6 cracked ice cubes, dash of sugar syrup (see page 9), 1 measure slivovitz, 1 measure apple brandy, 1 measure gin, 1 measure orange juice

1 Put the cracked ice cubes into a cocktail shaker. Dash the sugar syrup over the ice and pour in the slivovitz, apple brandy, gin, and orange juice. Shake vigorously until a frost forms.

2 Strain into a chilled cocktail glass.

FRUIT BRANDY COCKTAILS

CADIZ: put 4–6 cracked ice cubes into a cocktail shaker. Pour 1 measure blackberry brandy, 1½ measures dry sherry, ½ measure triple sec, and ½ measure light cream over the ice. Shake vigorously until a frost forms, then strain into a small, chilled glass.

CHI-CHI: half fill a chilled glass with cracked ice cubes. Pour 2 measures rum and 4 measures pineapple juice over the ice and stir to mix. Float ½ measure blackberry brandy on top by pouring it gently over the back of a teaspoon.

VANITY FAIR: put 4–6 cracked ice cubes into a cocktail shaker. Pour 2 measures apple brandy, 1 measure cherry brandy, and ½ measure Maraschino over the ice. Shake vigorously until a frost forms. Strain into a chilled cocktail glass and float 1 tablespoon amaretto on top by pouring it gently over the back of a teaspoon.

TULIP: put 4–6 cracked ice cubes into a cocktail shaker. Pour 1 measure apple brandy, 1 measure sweet vermouth, ½ measure apricot brandy, and ½ measure lemon juice over the ice. Shake vigorously until a frost forms, then strain into a chilled cocktail glass.

twin peaks

Bourbon, named after a county in Kentucky, must be made from at least 51 percent corn mash and is America's most popular whiskey. It forms the basis of many more cocktails than its Scotch cousin.

SERVES 1

4–6 cracked ice cubes, dash of triple sec, 2 measures bourbon,

1 measure Bénédictine, 1 measure lime juice, slice of lime, to decorate

1 Put the cracked ice cubes into a cocktail shaker. Dash triple sec over the ice and pour in the bourbon, Bénédictine, and lime juice. Shake vigorously until a frost forms.

2 Strain into a chilled highball glass and decorate with a slice of lime.

VARIATIONS

CONFEDERATE RAILROAD: put 4–6 cracked ice cubes into a cocktail shaker. Dash triple sec over the ice and pour in 2 measures bourbon, 1 measure Southern Comfort, and 1 measure orange juice. Shake vigorously until a frost forms, then strain into a chilled cocktail glass. Decorate with a slice of orange.

QUEEN OF MEMPHIS: put 4–6 cracked ice cubes into a cocktail shaker. Dash Maraschino over the ice and pour in 2 measures bourbon, 1 measure Midori, and 1 measure peach juice. Shake vigorously until a frost forms. Strain into a chilled cocktail glass and decorate with a wedge of melon.

TRASHY WOMEN: put 4–6 cracked ice cubes into a cocktail shaker. Dash Angostura bitters over the ice and pour in 2 measures bourbon, 1 measure Pernod, and 1 measure apple juice. Shake vigorously until a frost forms. Strain into a chilled cocktail glass and decorate with a slice of apple.

LONG GONE: put 4–6 cracked ice cubes into a cocktail shaker. Dash orange bitters over the ice and pour in 2 measures bourbon, 1 measure Drambuie, and 1 measure orange juice. Shake vigorously until a frost forms, then strain into a chilled cocktail glass. Decorate with a slice of orange.

irish shillelagh

A shillelagh (pronounced shee-lay-lee) is a wooden cudgel, traditionally made from blackthorn. Undoubtedly, this is a cocktail that hits the spot.

SERVES 1

4–6 crushed ice cubes,

2 measures Irish whiskey, 1 measure lemon juice,

½ measure sloe gin, ½ measure white rum, ½ tsp sugar syrup (see page 9),

½ peach, peeled, pitted, and finely chopped, 2 raspberries, to decorate

1 Put the crushed ice cubes into a blender and add the whiskey, lemon juice, sloe gin, rum, sugar syrup, and chopped peach. Blend until smooth.

2 Pour into a small, chilled highball glass and decorate with raspberries.

THE CRAÍC

SHILLELAGH: put 4–6 cracked ice cubes into a cocktail shaker. Pour 2 measures Irish whiskey, 1 measure dry sherry, 1 teaspoon golden rum, and 1 teaspoon lemon juice over the ice, and add a pinch of superfine sugar. Shake vigorously until a frost forms. Strain into a chilled cocktail glass and decorate with a cocktail cherry.

BLACKTHORN BUSH: put 4–6 cracked ice cubes into a mixing glass. Dash Pernod and Angostura bitters over the ice and pour in 1 measure Irish whiskey and 1 measure dry vermouth. Stir well to mix, then strain into a chilled cocktail glass.

IRISH AYES: put 4–6 cracked ice cubes into a mixing glass. Pour 2 measures Irish whiskey and ½ measure green Chartreuse over the ice. Stir well to mix, then strain into a chilled cocktail glass.

DID YOU KNOW?

Irish whiskey is never blended and must be matured for a minimum of five years.

cowboy

In movies, cowboys drink their rye straight, often pulling the cork out of the bottle with their teeth, and it is certainly difficult to imagine John Wayne or Clint Eastwood sipping delicately from a chilled cocktail glass.

SERVES 1

4–6 cracked ice cubes, 3 measures rye whiskey, 2 tbsp light cream

1 Put the cracked ice cubes into a cocktail shaker. Pour the whiskey and cream over the ice. Shake vigorously until a frost forms.

2 Strain into a chilled highball glass.

HOME ON THE RANGE

COWGIRL'S PRAYER: half fill a tall glass with cracked ice. Pour 2 measures golden tequila and 1 measure lime juice over the ice and top off with lemonade. Stir gently to mix and decorate with slices of lemon and lime.

OK CORRAL: put 4–6 cracked ice cubes into a cocktail shaker. Pour 2 measures rye whiskey, 1 measure grapefruit juice, and 1 teaspoon orgeat over the ice, and shake vigorously until a frost forms. Strain into a chilled cocktail glass.

NAVAJO TRAIL: put 4–6 cracked ice cubes into a cocktail shaker. Pour 2 measures white tequila, 1 measure triple sec, 1 measure lime juice, and 1 measure cranberry juice over the ice, and shake vigorously until a frost forms. Strain into a chilled cocktail glass.

KLONDIKE COOLER: put ½ teaspoon superfine sugar into a tall, chilled glass and add 1 measure ginger ale. Stir until the sugar has dissolved, then fill the glass with cracked ice cubes. Pour 2 measures blended American whiskey over the ice and top off with sparkling mineral water. Stir gently to mix and decorate with a spiral of lemon peel.

cat's eye

A cat's eye is many things—besides what a cat sees with—including a semi-precious stone and a stripy marble. Now, it's a highly potent cocktail, as pretty as a gemstone and certainly more fun than playing marbles.

SERVES 1

4–6 cracked ice cubes, 2 measures gin, 1½ measures dry vermouth,

½ measure kirsch, ½ measure triple sec, ½ measure lemon juice, ½ measure water

1 Put the cracked ice cubes into a cocktail shaker. Pour the gin, vermouth, kirsch, triple sec, lemon juice, and water over the ice.

2 Shake vigorously until a frost forms. Strain into a chilled goblet.

A WALK ON THE WILD SIDE

CHESHIRE CAT: put 4–6 cracked ice cubes into a mixing glass. Pour 1 measure brandy, 1 measure sweet vermouth, and 1 measure orange juice over the ice. Stir well to mix, then strain into a chilled champagne flute and top off with chilled champagne. Squeeze over a twist of orange peel and decorate with an orange peel spiral.

TIGER BY THE TAIL: put 4–6 crushed ice cubes into a blender and add 2 measures Pernod, 4 measures orange juice, and ¼ teaspoon triple sec. Blend until smooth, then pour into a chilled wine glass. Decorate with a wedge of lime.

RED LION: put 4–6 cracked ice cubes into a cocktail shaker. Dash grenadine over the ice and pour in 2 measures Grand Marnier, 1 measure gin, 1 measure orange juice, and 1 measure lemon juice over the ice. Shake vigorously until a frost forms, then strain into a chilled cocktail glass.

WHITE LION: put 4–6 cracked ice cubes into a cocktail shaker. Dash Angostura bitters and grenadine over the ice and pour in 2 measures white rum, 1 measure lemon juice, and 1 teaspoon sugar syrup (see page 9). Shake vigorously until a frost forms. Strain into a chilled cocktail glass.

road runner

Whether it is named after the real bird or after Bugs Bunny's famous companion, this is a cocktail for slowing down after a fast-moving day, not for speeding up the pace.

SERVES 1

4–6 cracked ice cubes, 2 measures gin, ½ measure dry vermouth,

½ measure Pernod, 1 tsp grenadine

1 Put the cracked ice into a cocktail shaker. Pour the gin, vermouth, Pernod, and grenadine over the ice. Shake vigorously until a frost forms.

2 Strain into a chilled wine glass.

VARIATIONS

FOX TROT: put 4–6 cracked ice cubes into a cocktail shaker. Dash Angostura bitters over the ice and pour in 2 measures white rum and 1 teaspoon lime juice. Shake vigorously until a frost forms, then strain into a chilled cocktail glass.

OCTOPUS'S GARDEN: Put 4–6 cracked ice cubes into a cocktail shaker. Pour 3 measures gin and 1 measure dry vermouth over the ice. Shake vigorously until a frost forms, then strain into a chilled cocktail glass. Decorate with a black olive and a smoked baby octopus.

ELK'S OWN: put 4–6 cracked ice cubes into a cocktail shaker. Pour 2 measures rye whiskey, 1 measure ruby port, ½ measure lemon juice, and 1 teaspoon sugar syrup (see page 9) over the ice, and add 1 egg white. Shake vigorously until a frost forms, then strain into a chilled cocktail glass, and decorate with a pineapple wedge.

RATTLESNAKE: pour 1 measure chilled Bailey's Irish Cream into a shot glass. With a steady hand, gently pour in 1 measure chilled, dark crème de cacao to make a second layer, then gently pour in 1 measure chilled Kahlúa to make a third layer. Do not stir.

SHARK ATTACK: half fill a tall, chilled glass with cracked ice cubes. Dash grenadine over the ice and pour in 3 measures vodka and 1½ measures lemonade. Stir gently.

breakfast

It is difficult to believe that anyone would actually have the stomach to cope with cocktails first thing in the morning—but then, for those who party all night and sleep all day, cocktail time coincides with breakfast.

SERVES 1

4–6 cracked ice cubes, 2 measures gin, 1 measure grenadine, 1 egg yolk

1 Put the cracked ice cubes into a cocktail shaker. Pour the gin and grenadine over the ice and add the egg yolk. Shake vigorously until a frost forms.

2 Strain into a chilled cocktail glass.

MEALTIMES

BREAKFAST EGG NOG: put 4–6 cracked ice cubes into a cocktail shaker. Pour 1 measure brandy, 1 measure clear Curaçao, and 3 measures chilled milk over the ice, and add 1 egg. Shake vigorously until a frost forms, then strain into a chilled glass.

LUPY'S LUNCHTIME PICK-ME-UP: put 4–6 crushed ice cubes into a blender and add 1½ measures Armagnac, 1 measure triple sec, ⅔ cup light cream, 1 teaspoon amaretto, and 1 egg. Blend until combined, then strain into a glass.

APERITIVO: put 4–6 cracked ice cubes into a mixing glass. Dash orange bitters over the ice and pour in 2 measures gin and 1½ measures white Sambuca. Stir well to mix, then strain into a chilled cocktail glass.

AFTER DINNER: put 4–6 cracked ice cubes into a cocktail shaker. Pour 1 measure apricot brandy, 1 measure triple sec, and 1 measure lime juice over the ice. Shake vigorously until a frost forms, then strain into a chilled cocktail glass.

AFTER SUPPER: put 4–6 cracked ice cubes into a cocktail shaker. Pour 1 measure apricot brandy, 1 measure triple sec, and 1 measure lemon juice over the ice. Shake vigorously until a frost forms, then strain into a chilled cocktail glass.

Cocktails and Punches

suffering fool

You will have to make up your own mind whether this cocktail is a cure for someone already suffering or whether it is the cause of suffering still to come.

SERVES 1

1 tbsp Angostura bitters, 6–8 cracked ice cubes, 2 measures gin,

1½ measures brandy, ½ measure lime juice,

1 tsp sugar syrup (see page 9), ginger beer, to top off,

slice of cucumber, slice of lime, sprig of fresh mint, to decorate

1 Pour the Angostura bitters into a chilled Collins glass and swirl around, until the inside of the glass is coated. Pour out the excess and discard.

2 Half fill the glass with cracked ice cubes. Pour the gin, brandy, lime juice, and sugar syrup over the ice. Stir well to mix.

3 Top off with ginger beer and stir gently. Decorate with the cucumber and lime slices and a mint sprig.

OTHER "PAINFUL" COCKTAILS

ANKLE BREAKER: put 4–6 cracked ice cubes into a cocktail shaker. Pour 2 measures dark rum, 1 measure cherry brandy, 1 measure lime juice, and 1 teaspoon sugar syrup (see page 9) over the ice. Shake until a frost forms, then strain into a small, chilled glass.

THIRD DEGREE: put 4–6 cracked ice cubes into a mixing glass. Dash Pernod over the ice and pour in 2 measures gin and 1 measure dry vermouth. Stir well to mix, then strain into a chilled cocktail glass.

BARBED WIRE: put 4–6 cracked ice cubes into a cocktail shaker. Pour 3 measures vodka, 1 teaspoon sweet vermouth, ½ teaspoon Pernod, and ½ measure dry sherry over the ice. Shake until a frost forms. Strain into a chilled cocktail glass and decorate with a twist of lemon peel.

nirvana

It may not be possible to obtain a perfect state of harmony and bliss through a cocktail, but this has to be the next best thing.

SERVES 1

8–10 cracked ice cubes, 2 measures dark rum, ½ measure grenadine,

½ measure tamarind syrup, 1 tsp sugar syrup (see page 9),

grapefruit juice, to top off

1 Put 4–6 cracked ice cubes into a cocktail shaker. Pour the rum, grenadine, tamarind syrup, and sugar syrup over the ice and shake vigorously until a frost forms.

2 Half fill a chilled Collins glass with cracked ice cubes and strain the cocktail over them. Top off with grapefruit juice.

HEAVENLY BLISS

PARADISE: put 4–6 cracked ice cubes into a cocktail shaker. Pour 2 measures apricot brandy, 1 measure gin, 1½ measures orange juice, and ½ teaspoon grenadine over the ice. Shake vigorously until a frost forms. Strain into a chilled cocktail glass.

HEAVENLY: put 4–6 cracked ice cubes into a mixing glass. Pour 1½ measures brandy, ½ measure cherry brandy, and ½ measure plum brandy over the ice, and stir well to mix. Strain into a chilled cocktail glass.

SEVENTH HEAVEN: put 4–6 cracked ice cubes into a cocktail shaker. Pour 2 measures gin, ½ measure Maraschino, and ½ measure grapefruit juice over the ice. Shake vigorously until a frost forms, then strain into a chilled cocktail glass. Decorate with a sprig of fresh mint.

AMBROSIA: put 4–6 cracked ice cubes into a cocktail shaker. Pour 1½ measures brandy, 1½ measures apple brandy, and ½ teaspoon raspberry syrup over the ice. Shake vigorously until a frost forms and strain into a chilled wine glass. Top off with chilled champagne and decorate with a raspberry.

Cocktails and Punches

cinderella

If the fairy-story heroine had been knocking back cocktails until the clock struck midnight, it's hardly surprising that she forgot the time, mislaid her pumpkin, and lost her shoe on the way home.

SERVES 1

4–6 cracked ice cubes, 3 measures white rum, 1 measure white port, 1 measure lemon juice, 1 tsp sugar syrup (see page 9), 1 egg white

1 Put the cracked ice cubes into a cocktail shaker. Pour the rum, port, lemon juice, and sugar syrup over the ice and add the egg white.

2 Shake vigorously until a frost forms and strain into a chilled glass.

AND THEY ALL LIVED HAPPILY EVER AFTER

GLASS SLIPPER: put 4–6 cracked ice cubes into a cocktail shaker. Pour 3 measures gin and 1 measure blue Curaçao over the ice. Shake vigorously until a frost forms, then strain into a chilled cocktail glass.

PRINCE CHARMING: put 4–6 cracked ice cubes into a cocktail shaker. Pour 2 measures vodka, 1 measure apricot brandy, 1 measure apple brandy, and 1 teaspoon lemon juice over the ice. Shake vigorously until a frost forms, then strain into a chilled cocktail glass.

PETER PAN: put 4–6 cracked ice cubes into a cocktail shaker. Pour 1 measure gin, 1 measure dry vermouth, 1 measure peach brandy, and 1 measure orange juice over the ice. Shake until a frost forms, then strain into a chilled cocktail glass.

TINKERBELL: put 4–6 cracked ice cubes into a cocktail shaker. Dash grenadine over the ice, pour in 2 measures vodka and 1 measure cherry brandy, and add 1 egg white. Shake vigorously until a frost forms, then strain into a chilled cocktail glass.

palm beach

If it's been a long time since your last vacation, conjure up the blue skies of Florida and the rolling surf with this sunny cocktail.

SERVES 1

4–6 cracked ice cubes, 1 measure white rum,

1 measure gin, 1 measure pineapple juice

1 Put the cracked ice into a cocktail shaker. Pour the rum, gin, and pineapple juice over the ice. Shake vigorously until a frost forms.

2 Strain into a chilled highball glass.

TAKING TIME OUT

MIAMI BEACH: put 4–6 cracked ice cubes into a cocktail shaker. Pour 2 measures Scotch whisky, 1½ measures dry vermouth, and 2 measures grapefruit juice over the ice. Shake vigorously until a frost forms, then strain into a chilled cocktail glass.

FLORIDA: put 4–6 cracked ice cubes into a cocktail shaker. Pour 1 measure gin, 1 teaspoon triple sec, 1 teaspoon kirsch, and 2 measures orange juice over the ice. Shake vigorously until a frost forms, then strain into a chilled cocktail glass.

BERMUDA BLOOM: put 4–6 cracked ice cubes into a cocktail shaker. Dash triple sec over the ice and pour in 1 measure gin, 1 measure lemon juice, 1 measure orange juice, ½ measure apricot brandy, and 1 teaspoon sugar syrup (see page 9). Shake vigorously until a frost forms, then strain into a chilled cocktail glass.

DEAUVILLE: put 4–6 cracked ice cubes into a cocktail shaker. Pour 1½ measures brandy, 1 measure apple brandy, ½ measure triple sec, and ½ measure lemon juice over the ice. Shake vigorously until a frost forms, then strain into a chilled glass.

COSTA DEL SOL: put 4–6 cracked ice cubes into a cocktail shaker. Pour 2 measures gin, 1 measure apricot brandy, and 1 measure triple sec over the ice. Shake vigorously until a frost forms, then strain into a chilled cocktail glass.

Cocktails and Punches

bishop

It is strange how men of the cloth have gained a reputation for being enthusiastic about the good, material things in life. Even Rudyard Kipling wrote about smuggling "brandy for the parson." It goes to show that spirituality is no barrier to spirits.

SERVES 1

4–6 cracked ice cubes, dash of lemon juice, 1 measure white rum,

1 tsp red wine, pinch of superfine sugar

1 Put the cracked ice cubes into a cocktail shaker. Dash the lemon juice over the ice, pour in the white rum and red wine, and add a pinch of sugar. Shake vigorously until a frost forms.

2 Strain into a chilled wine glass.

INTERDENOMINATIONAL COCKTAILS

PRESBYTERIAN: half fill a glass with cracked ice cubes. Pour 3 measures bourbon, 3 measures ginger ale, and 3 measures sparkling mineral water over the ice. Stir gently.

PARISH PRIEST: put 4–6 cracked ice cubes into a cocktail shaker. Dash triple sec, Pernod, and orange bitters over the ice, and pour in 2 measures Irish whiskey and 1 measure sweet vermouth. Shake vigorously until a frost forms, then strain into a chilled cocktail glass.

CURATE'S EGG: put 4–6 crushed ice cubes into a blender and add 2 measures brandy, 1 measure Tia Maria, 1 measure sweet sherry, 3/4 cup light cream, 1 teaspoon sugar syrup (see page 9), and 1 egg. Blend until smooth, then pour into a tall, chilled glass.

QUAKER'S: put 4–6 cracked ice cubes into a cocktail shaker. Pour 1 measure brandy, 1 measure white rum, ½ measure lemon juice, and ½ measure raspberry syrup over the ice. Shake vigorously until a frost forms, then strain into a chilled cocktail glass.

PURITAN: put 4–6 cracked ice cubes into a cocktail shaker. Dash apricot brandy and orange juice over the ice and pour in 1 measure gin and 1 measure Lillet. Shake vigorously until a frost forms, then strain into a chilled cocktail glass.

el diablo

One or two El Diablos and you will certainly feel a bit of a devil, but one or two too many and you will feel like the very devil!

SERVES 1

6–8 cracked ice cubes, 2–3 strips of lime peel, 1 measure lime juice, 3 measures white tequila, 1 measure crème de cassis

1 Fill a small, chilled glass with cracked ice cubes and add the lime peel.

2 Pour the lime juice over the ice and add the tequila and crème de cassis.

DEVILISH DRINKS

DIABLO: put 4–6 cracked ice cubes into a cocktail shaker. Dash lemon juice over the ice and pour in 2 measures white port and 1 measure dry vermouth. Shake until a frost forms. Strain into a chilled glass and decorate with a lemon peel twist.

DEVIL'S COCKTAIL: put 4–6 cracked ice cubes into a mixing glass. Dash lemon juice over the ice and pour in 2 measures ruby port and 1 measure dry vermouth. Stir well. Strain the mixture into a chilled cocktail glass. Decorate with a lemon peel twist.

BLACK DEVIL: put 4–6 cracked ice cubes into a mixing glass. Pour 2 measures white rum and ½ measure dry vermouth over the ice and then stir well to mix. Strain into a chilled cocktail glass and decorate with a pitted black olive.

BLUE DEVIL: put 4–6 cracked ice cubes into a cocktail shaker. Pour 2 measures gin, ½ measure lime juice, 1 tablespoon Maraschino, and 1 teaspoon blue Curaçao over the ice. Shake until a frost forms. Strain into a chilled cocktail glass.

DID YOU KNOW?

Tequila is a secondary product of the agave plant, which was originally used to produce pulque, a fermented, milky liquor. Pulque is reputed to taste quite disgusting and, although it was popular with native Mexicans, Spanish colonists preferred to distil it to produce tequila.

huatusco whammer

To be authentic, this cocktail should be topped off with Coca-Cola®, but you can use other brands of cola if you prefer. Make sure that the cola is well chilled.

SERVES 1

8–10 cracked ice cubes, 1 measure white tequila, ½ measure white rum, ½ measure vodka, ½ measure gin, ½ measure triple sec, 1 measure lemon juice, ½ tsp sugar syrup (see page 9), cola, to top off

1 Put 4–6 cracked ice cubes into a cocktail shaker. Pour the tequila, rum, vodka, gin, triple sec, lemon juice, and sugar syrup over the ice. Shake vigorously until a frost forms.

2 Fill a chilled Collins glass with cracked ice cubes and strain the cocktail over them. Top off with cola, stir gently, and serve with straws.

VARIATIONS

MEXICOLA: half fill a tall, chilled glass with cracked ice cubes. Pour 2 measures tequila and 1 measure lime juice over the ice and top off with cola. Stir gently and decorate the glass with a slice of lime.

CHERRYCOLA: half fill a tall, chilled glass with cracked ice. Pour 2 measures cherry brandy and 1 measure lemon juice over the ice. Top off with cola, stir gently, and decorate with a slice of lemon.

LOUNGE LIZARD: half fill a tall, chilled glass with cracked ice cubes. Add 2 measures dark rum and 1 measure amaretto. Top off with cola and stir.

tequila mockingbird

In spite of the horrible literary pun in the name, this popular cocktail is fast becoming a modern classic.

SERVES 1

4–6 cracked ice cubes,

2 measures white tequila,

1 measure white crème de menthe,

1 measure fresh lime juice

1 Put the cracked ice cubes into a cocktail shaker. Add the tequila, crème de menthe, and lime juice.

2 Strain into a chilled highball glass.

STRICTLY FOR THE BIRDS

BIRD OF PARADISE: put 4–6 cracked ice cubes into a cocktail shaker. Pour 1½ measures white tequila, ½ measure white creme de cacao, ½ measure Galliano, 1 measure orange juice, and ½ measure light cream over the ice. Shake vigorously until a frost forms, then strain into a chilled wine glass.

BLUE BIRD: put 4–6 cracked ice cubes into a cocktail shaker. Dash Angostura bitters over the ice and pour in 3 measures gin and 1 measure blue Curaçao. Shake vigorously until a frost forms, then strain into a chilled cocktail glass.

DID YOU KNOW?

Crème de menthe, just about the only liqueur flavored with a single herb rather than a mixture, was always colored green when it was first produced. Nowadays, white crème de menthe, which is no different in flavor, is widely available.

wild night out

Tequila has a reputation for being an extraordinarily potent spirit, but most commercially exported brands are the same standard strength as other spirits, such as gin or whiskey. "Home-grown" tequila or its close relative, mescal, may be quite another matter.

SERVES 1

4–6 cracked ice cubes, 3 measures white tequila,

2 measures cranberry juice, 1 measure lime juice, club soda, to top off

1 Put the cracked ice cubes into a cocktail shaker. Pour the tequila, cranberry juice, and lime juice over the ice. Shake vigorously until a frost forms.

2 Half fill a chilled highball glass with cracked ice cubes and strain the cocktail over them. Add club soda to taste.

THE WILD BUNCH

BUTTAFUOCO: put 4–6 cracked ice cubes into a cocktail shaker. Pour 2 measures white tequila, ½ measure Galliano, ½ measure cherry brandy, and ½ measure lemon juice over the ice. Shake vigorously until a frost forms. Half fill a glass with cracked ice cubes and strain the cocktail over them. Top off with club soda and decorate with a cocktail cherry.

MAGNA CARTA: rub the rim of a wine glass with a wedge of lime, then dip in a saucer of superfine sugar to frost. Put 4–6 cracked ice cubes into a mixing glass. Pour 2 measures white tequila and 1 measure triple sec over the ice and stir well to mix. Strain into the prepared glass and top off with chilled sparkling wine.

TEQUILA FIZZ: put 4–6 cracked ice cubes into a cocktail shaker. Pour 3 measures white tequila, 1 measure grenadine, and 1 measure lime juice over the ice and add 1 egg white. Shake vigorously until a frost forms. Half fill a chilled glass with cracked ice cubes and strain the cocktail over them. Top off with ginger ale.

carolina

White tequila is most commonly used for mixing cocktails, but some require the mellower flavor of the amber-colored, aged tequilas, which are known as golden tequila or *añejo*.

SERVES 1

4–6 cracked ice cubes, 3 measures golden tequila, 1 tsp grenadine,

1 tsp vanilla extract, 1 measure light cream, 1 egg white,

ground cinnamon, cocktail cherry, to decorate

1 Put the cracked ice cubes into a cocktail shaker. Pour the tequila, grenadine, vanilla, and cream over the ice and add the egg white. Shake vigorously until a frost forms.

2 Strain into a chilled cocktail glass. Sprinkle with cinnamon and decorate with a cocktail cherry.

THE GOLDEN TOUCH

GRAPESHOT: put 4–6 cracked ice cubes into a cocktail shaker. Pour 2 measures golden tequila, 1 measure clear Curaçao, and 1½ measures white grape juice over the ice and shake vigorously until a frost forms. Strain into a chilled cocktail glass.

CHAPALA: put 4–6 cracked ice cubes into a cocktail shaker. Pour 2 measures golden tequila, 2 measures orange juice, 1 measure lime juice, ½ measure triple sec, and ½ measure grenadine over the ice. Shake vigorously until a frost forms. Half fill a chilled glass with cracked ice cubes and strain the cocktail over them.

PIÑATA: put 4–6 cracked ice cubes into a cocktail shaker and add 2 measures golden tequila, 1 measure crème de banane, and 1½ measures lime juice. Shake until a frost forms. Strain into a chilled glass.

MONTEZUMA: put 4–6 crushed ice cubes into a blender and add 2 measures golden tequila, 1 measure Madeira, and 1 egg yolk. Blend until smooth, then pour into a chilled cocktail glass.

Cocktails and Punches

chile willy

Truly a cocktail for the brave-hearted—the heat depends on the type of chile, since some are much more fiery than others, as well as the quantity you add and whether the chile was seeded first. For an even spicier cocktail, use chile vodka instead of plain.

SERVES 1

4–6 cracked ice cubes, 2 measures vodka, 1 tsp chopped fresh chile

1 Put the ice into a cocktail shaker. Pour the vodka over the ice and add the chile.

2 Shake until a frost forms and strain into a chilled glass.

FLAVORED VODKAS

KUCH BEHAR: put 6–8 cracked ice cubes into a chilled glass. Pour 1 measure pepper vodka and 1 measure tomato juice over the ice. Stir well to mix.

HOT AND DIRTY MARTINI: put 4–6 cracked ice cubes into a cocktail shaker. Pour 3 measures pepper vodka, ½ measure dry vermouth, and 1 teaspoon olive brine over the ice. Shake until a frost forms. Strain into a chilled cocktail glass. Decorate with a stuffed olive. (For a Martini and other variations, see page 25.)

FUZZY MARTINI: put 4–6 cracked ice cubes into a cocktail shaker. Pour 2 measures vanilla vodka, ½ measure coffee vodka, and 1 teaspoon peach schnapps over the ice. Shake until a frost forms. Strain into a chilled cocktail glass and decorate with a slice of peach. (For a Martini and other variations, see page 25.)

STOCKHOLM: put a sugar lump in a goblet and add 2 measures lemon vodka, and 1 measure lemon juice. Stir until thoroughly dissolved. Top off with chilled sparkling wine.

crocodile

This is certainly a snappy cocktail with a bit of bite. However, it probably gets its name from its spectacular color—Midori, a Japanese melon-flavored liqueur, is a startling shade of green.

SERVES 1

4–6 cracked ice cubes, 2 measures vodka, 1 measure triple sec,

1 measure Midori, 2 measures lemon juice

1 Put the cracked ice cubes into a cocktail shaker. Pour the vodka, triple sec, Midori, and lemon juice over the ice. Shake vigorously until a frost forms.

2 Strain into a chilled cocktail glass.

VARIATIONS

ALLIGATOR: put 4–6 cracked ice cubes into a cocktail shaker. Pour 2 measures vodka, 1 measure Midori, ½ measure dry vermouth, and ¼ teaspoon lemon juice over the ice. Shake vigorously until a frost forms. Strain into a chilled cocktail glass.

MELON BALL: put 4–6 cracked ice cubes into a mixing glass. Pour 2 measures vodka, 2 measures Midori, and 4 measures pineapple juice over the ice and stir well to mix. Half fill a chilled glass with cracked ice cubes and strain the cocktail over them. Decorate with a melon wedge.

MELON BALLS: put 4–6 cracked ice cubes into a cocktail shaker. Pour 1 measure vodka, 1 measure Midori, and 1 measure pineapple juice over the ice. Shake vigorously until a frost forms, then strain into a chilled cocktail glass.

MELON STATE BALLS: put 4–6 cracked ice cubes into a cocktail shaker. Pour 2 measures vodka, 1 measure Midori, and 2 measures orange juice over the ice. Shake vigorously until a frost forms, then strain the mixture into a chilled cocktail glass.

Cocktails and Punches

fuzzy navel

This is another one of those cocktails with a name that plays on the ingredients—fuzzy to remind you that it contains peach schnapps and navel because it is mixed with orange juice. It is no reflection on anyone's personal hygiene.

SERVES 1

4–6 cracked ice cubes, 2 measures vodka, 1 measure peach schnapps,

1 cup orange juice, slice of orange, to decorate

1 Put the cracked ice cubes into a cocktail shaker. Pour the vodka, peach schnapps, and orange juice over the ice. Shake vigorously until a frost forms.

2 Strain into a chilled glass and decorate with a slice of orange.

VARIATIONS

HALLEY'S COMFORT: half fill a tall, chilled glass with cracked ice cubes. Pour 2 measures Southern Comfort and 2 measures peach schnapps over the ice and top off with sparkling mineral water. Stir and decorate with a slice of lemon.

WOO-WOO: half fill a chilled glass with cracked ice. Pour 2 measures vodka, 2 measures peach schnapps and 4 measures cranberry juice over the ice. Stir well.

ROYAL WEDDING: put 4–6 cracked ice cubes into a cocktail shaker. Pour 1 measure kirsch, 1 measure peach brandy, and 1 measure orange juice over the ice. Shake vigorously until a frost forms, then strain into a chilled cocktail glass.

SOUTHERN PEACH: put 4–6 cracked ice cubes into a cocktail shaker. Dash Angostura bitters over the ice and pour in 1 measure Southern Comfort, 1 measure peach brandy, and 1 measure light cream. Shake vigorously until a frost forms, then strain into a chilled cocktail glass. Decorate with a slice of peach.

mudslide

This ominous-sounding cocktail is actually a gorgeously creamy and richly-flavored concoction that is delicious whatever the weather conditions.

SERVES 1

4–6 cracked ice cubes, 1½ measures Kahlúa,

1½ measures Bailey's Irish Cream, 1½ measures vodka

1 Put the cracked ice cubes into a cocktail shaker. Pour the Kahlúa, Bailey's Irish Cream, and vodka over the ice. Shake vigorously until a frost forms.

2 Strain into a chilled goblet.

METEOROLOGICAL MIXES

DARK AND STORMY: half fill a chilled glass with cracked ice cubes. Pour 1 measure dark rum and 2 measures ginger beer over the ice and stir gently.

COOL WIND: put 4–6 cracked ice cubes into a mixing glass. Pour 3 measures vodka, 1 measure dry vermouth, 1 measure grapefruit juice, and ½ teaspoon triple sec over the ice. Stir well to mix, then strain into a chilled cocktail glass.

FAIR AND WARMER: put 4–6 cracked ice cubes into a glass. Dash clear Curaçao over the ice. Pour in 2 measures white rum and 1 measure sweet vermouth. Stir, then strain into a chilled cocktail glass.

CLEAR SKIES AHEAD: put 4–6 cracked ice cubes into a cocktail shaker. Pour 2 measures Scotch whisky, 1 measure lemon juice, ½ teaspoon sugar syrup (see page 9), and ½ teaspoon grenadine over the ice, and add 1 egg white. Shake vigorously until a frost forms, then strain into a chilled cocktail glass.

DAMN THE WEATHER: put 4–6 cracked ice cubes into a cocktail shaker. Pour 2 measures gin, ½ measure orange juice, 1 tablespoon sweet vermouth, and 2 teaspoons triple sec over the ice. Shake vigorously until a frost forms, then strain into a chilled cocktail glass.

Cocktails and Punches

godfather

Amaretto is an Italian liqueur, so perhaps the inspiration for this cocktail comes from Don Corleone, the eponymous character in Mario Puzo's best-selling novel, unforgettably portrayed in the movie by Marlon Brando.

SERVES 1

4–6 cracked ice cubes, 2 measures Scotch whisky, 1 measure amaretto

1 Fill a chilled highball glass with cracked ice cubes. Pour in the whisky and amaretto and stir to mix.

THE FAMILY

GODMOTHER: put 4–6 cracked ice cubes into a small, chilled glass. Pour 2 measures vodka and 1 measure amaretto over the ice. Stir to mix.

GODCHILD: put 4–6 crushed ice cubes into a blender and add 1½ measures amaretto, 1 measure vodka, and 1 measure light cream. Blend until smooth, then pour into a chilled champagne flute.

GODDAUGHTER: put 4–6 crushed ice cubes into a blender and add 2 measures apple brandy, 1 measure amaretto, and 1 tablespoon apple sauce. Blend until smooth, then pour the mixture, without straining, into a chilled goblet. Sprinkle with ground cinnamon and serve with a straw.

DID YOU KNOW?

Although flavored with almonds and herbal extracts, amaretto is actually made from apricot kernels.

freedom fighter

Crème Yvette is an American liqueur flavored with Parma violets. Because it has such a distinctive taste, you either love it or hate it—but it certainly makes pretty cocktails because it is such a lovely color. You could also use crème de violette, which is similar although not identical.

SERVES 1

4–6 cracked ice cubes, 3 measures sloe gin,

1 measure Crème Yvette, 1 measure lemon juice, 1 egg white

1 Put the cracked ice cubes into a cocktail shaker. Pour the gin, Crème Yvette, and lemon juice over the ice, and add the egg white. Shake vigorously until a frost forms.

2 Strain into a chilled wine glass.

VARIATIONS

PING PONG: put 4–6 cracked ice cubes into a cocktail shaker. Pour 1 measure Crème Yvette, 1 measure sloe gin, and ½ measure lemon juice over the ice. Shake vigorously until a frost forms, then pour into a chilled cocktail glass.

SNOWBALL: put 4–6 cracked ice cubes into a cocktail shaker. Pour 1½ measures gin, ½ measure Crème Yvette, ½ measure Anisette, ½ measure light cream, and ½ teaspoon sugar syrup (see page 9) over the ice. Shake vigorously until a frost forms, then pour into a chilled cocktail glass.

UNION JACK: put 4–6 cracked ice cubes into a cocktail shaker. Pour in 3 measures dry gin and 1 measure Crème Yvette. Shake vigorously until a frost forms, then strain into a chilled cocktail glass.

JUPITER: put 4–6 cracked ice cubes into a cocktail shaker. Pour 2 measures gin, 1 measure dry vermouth, ½ measure Crème Yvette, and ½ measure orange juice over the ice. Shake vigorously until a frost forms, then strain into a chilled wine glass.

banshee

A surprising number of cocktails are named after ghouls, ghosts, and things that go bump in the night. It seems unlikely that this one will get you wailing (except with delight), but it might make your hair stand on end.

SERVES 1

4–6 cracked ice cubes, 2 measures crème de banane,

1 measure crème de cacao, 1 measure light cream

1 Put the cracked ice cubes into a cocktail shaker. Pour the crème de banane, crème de cacao, and light cream over the ice. Shake vigorously until a frost forms.

2 Strain into a chilled wine glass.

SUPERNATURAL COCKTAILS

RED WITCH: put 4–6 cracked ice cubes into a cocktail shaker. Pour 2 measures Pernod and 1 measure blackcurrant cordial over the ice. Shake until a frost forms. Pour into a chilled wine glass and top off with chilled hard cider.

WHITE WITCH: put 4–6 cracked ice cubes into a cocktail shaker. Pour 2 measures white rum, 1 measure triple sec, and 1 measure white crème de cacao over the ice. Shake vigorously until a frost forms. Half fill a chilled glass with cracked ice cubes and strain the cocktail over them. Top off with sparkling mineral water.

ENCHANTMENT: put 4–6 cracked ice cubes into a cocktail shaker. Dash dry vermouth and orange bitters over the ice and pour in 2 measures Canadian whisky and 1 measure blue Curaçao. Shake vigorously until a frost forms, then strain into a chilled cocktail glass.

LEPRECHAUN: put 4–6 crushed ice cubes into a blender. Pour in 2 measures Irish whiskey, 1 measure white rum, 1 measure lemon juice, ½ measure sloe gin, ½ teaspoon sugar syrup (see page 9), and ¼ peeled, pitted, and sliced peach. Blend until slushy. Pour into a small, chilled glass and decorate with raspberries.

angel's delight

This is a modern version of the classic pousse café, an unmixed, mixed drink, in that the ingredients form separate layers in the glass—provided you have a steady hand—to create a rainbow effect. You can drink it as a slammer or sip it in a much more genteel manner.

SERVES 1

½ measure chilled grenadine, ½ measure chilled triple sec,

½ measure chilled sloe gin, ½ measure chilled light cream

1 Pour the grenadine into a chilled shot glass, pousse café glass, or champagne flute, then, with a steady hand, pour in the triple sec to make a second layer.

2 Add the sloe gin to make a third layer and, finally, add the cream to float on top.

VARIATIONS

ANGEL'S TIT: pour ½ measure chilled white crème de cacao into a chilled shot glass, pousse café glass, or champagne flute. With a steady hand, pour in ½ measure chilled Maraschino to make a second layer and, finally, pour in ½ measure light cream to float on top. Decorate with a cocktail cherry.

POUSSE CAFÉ: pour ½ measure chilled grenadine into chilled shot glass, pousse café glass, or champagne flute. With a steady hand, pour in ½ measure chilled white crème de cacao to make a second layer, followed by ½ measure chilled Maraschino to make a third layer. Pour in ½ measure chilled clear Curaçao, then pour in ½ measure chilled green crème de menthe to make a fifth layer. Finally, pour in ½ measure chilled brandy to float on top.

POUSSE L'AMOUR: pour ½ measure chilled Maraschino into a chilled shot glass, pousse café glass, or champagne flute, then, with a steady hand, add 1 egg yolk to make a second layer. Then pour in ½ measure chilled Bénédictine to make a third layer and, finally, pour in ½ measure chilled brandy to float on top.

Cocktails and Punches

full monty

The expression "full monty," meaning not holding anything back, has been around for a long time, but was given a new lease of life by the highly successful British movie of the same title. However, you can keep your clothes on when mixing and drinking this cocktail, but you might want to take them off when you've had a couple.

SERVES 1

4–6 cracked ice cubes, 1 measure vodka, 1 measure Galliano,

grated ginseng root, to decorate

1 Put the cracked ice cubes into a cocktail shaker. Pour the vodka and Galliano over the ice. Shake vigorously until a frost forms.

2 Strain into a chilled cocktail glass and sprinkle with grated ginseng root.

CINEMATIC COCKTAILS

BACK TO THE FUTURE: put 4–6 cracked ice cubes into a cocktail shaker. Pour 2 measures gin, 1 measure slivovitz, and 1 measure lemon juice over the ice. Shake vigorously until a frost forms. Strain into a chilled cocktail glass.

STAR WARS: put 4–6 cracked ice cubes into a cocktail shaker. Pour 2 measures gin, 2 measures lemon juice, 1 measure Galliano, and 1 measure crème de noyaux over the ice. Shake vigorously until a frost forms. Strain into a chilled cocktail glass.

TITANIC: put 4–6 cracked ice cubes into a cocktail shaker. Pour 3 measures Mandarine Napoléon and 2 measures vodka over the ice. Shake vigorously until a frost forms. Half fill a chilled glass with cracked ice cubes and strain the cocktail over them. Top off with sparkling mineral water.

LAST MANGO IN PARIS: put 4–6 cracked ice cubes into a blender and add 2 measures vodka, 1 measure crème de framboise, 1 measure lime juice, ½ peeled, pitted, and chopped mango, and 2 halved strawberries. Blend until slushy. Pour into a chilled goblet and decorate with a slice of lime and a strawberry.

star bangled spanner

Although only half measures of each spirit are used, there are seven layers of them, so this is quite a potent cocktail. It is probably fortunate that after getting your tongue around a couple, your hand will become too unsteady to pour more.

SERVES 1

½ measure chilled green Chartreuse, ½ measure chilled triple sec,

½ measure chilled cherry brandy, ½ measure chilled crème violette,

½ measure chilled yellow Chartreuse, ½ measure chilled blue Curaçao,

½ measure chilled brandy

1 Pour the green Chartreuse into a chilled champagne flute, then, with a steady hand, gently pour in the triple sec to make a second layer.

2 Gently add the cherry brandy to make a third layer, the crème violette to make a fourth, the yellow Chartreuse to make a fifth, and the Curaçao to make a sixth.

3 Finally, float the brandy on top.

FLY THE FLAG

STARS AND STRIPES: pour 3/4 measure chilled cherry brandy into a chilled shot glass, pousse café glass, or champagne flute. With a steady hand, gently pour in 1½ measures chilled light cream to make a second layer and, finally, gently pour in 3/4 measure chilled blue Curaçao.

UNION JACK: pour 1 measure chilled Maraschino into a chilled shot glass. With a steady hand, gently pour in 1 measure chilled blue Curaçao to make a second layer, and, finally, gently pour in 1 measure chilled grenadine.

TRICOLOR: pour 1 measure chilled green crème de menthe into a chilled shot glass. With a steady hand, gently pour in 1 measure chilled Bailey's Irish Cream to make a second layer and, finally, gently pour in 1 measure chilled red Maraschino.

Cocktails and Punches

m a d dog

This cocktail is named in honor of Maximum Dog, who is himself a cocktail of breeds and who has been described as a cross between a goat and a monkey. However, he is not allowed to drink it.

SERVES 1

4–6 cracked ice cubes, 1 measure white tequila, 1 measure crème de banane,

1 measure white crème de cacao, ½ measure lime juice,

slice of lime, slice of banana, cocktail cherry, to decorate

1 Put the cracked ice cubes into a cocktail shaker. Pour the tequila, crème de banane, crème de cacao, and lime juice over the ice. Shake vigorously until a frost forms.

2 Strain into a chilled cocktail glass and decorate with a lime slice, banana slice, and cocktail cherry.

CANINE COCKTAILS

BEAGLE: put 4–6 cracked ice cubes into a mixing glass. Dash kümmel and lemon juice over the ice and pour in 2 measures brandy and 1 measure cranberry juice. Stir well to mix, then strain into a chilled cocktail glass.

GREAT DANE: put 4–6 cracked ice cubes into a cocktail shaker. Pour 2 measures gin, 1 measure cherry brandy, ½ measure dry vermouth, and 1 teaspoon kirsch over the ice. Shake vigorously until a frost forms, then strain into a chilled cocktail glass. Decorate with a twist of lemon peel.

BLOODHOUND: put 4–6 crushed ice cubes into a blender and add 2 measures gin, 1 measure sweet vermouth, 1 measure dry vermouth, and 3 strawberries. Blend until smooth, then strain into a chilled cocktail glass.

BLACK DOG: put 4–6 cracked ice cubes into a mixing glass. Pour 3 measures bourbon, 1 measure dry vermouth, and ½ measure crème de cassis over the ice. Stir well to mix. Half fill a small, chilled glass with cracked ice cubes and strain the cocktail over them.

jade

You can tell good jade because it always feel cold to the touch—and that should apply to cocktails, too. No cocktail bar—whether in a hotel, pub, or at home—can ever have too much ice. Don't forget to chill the champagne for at least 2 hours before mixing.

SERVES 1

4–6 cracked ice cubes, dash of Angostura bitters, ¼ measure Midori,

¼ measure blue Curaçao, ¼ measure lime juice,

chilled champagne, to top off, slice of lime, to decorate

1 Put the cracked ice cubes into a cocktail shaker. Dash Angostura bitters over the ice and pour in the Midori, Curaçao, and lime juice. Shake vigorously until a frost forms.

2 Strain into a chilled champagne flute. Top off with chilled champagne and decorate with a slice of lime.

JEWELRY BOX

DIAMOND HEAD (to serve two): put 6–8 cracked ice cubes into a cocktail shaker. Pour 4 measures gin, 2 measures lemon juice, 1 measure apricot brandy, and 1 teaspoon sugar syrup (see page 9) over the ice, and add 1 egg white. Shake vigorously until a frost forms, then strain into two chilled cocktail glasses.

SAPPHIRE MARTINI: put 4–6 cracked ice cubes into a mixing glass. Pour 2 measures gin and ½ measure blue Curaçao over the ice. Stir well to mix, then strain into a chilled cocktail glass. Decorate with a blue cocktail cherry. (For a Martini and other variations, see page 25.)

TOPAZ MARTINI: put 4–6 cracked ice cubes into a mixing glass. Pour 2 measures gin and ½ measure orange Curaçao over the ice. Stir to mix. Strain into a chilled cocktail glass. Decorate with a slice of lemon.

EMERALD ISLE: put 4–6 cracked ice cubes into a mixing glass. Dash Angostura bitters over the ice and pour in 2½ measures gin and 2 teaspoons green crème de menthe. Stir well to mix, then strain into a chilled cocktail glass. Decorate with a green cocktail olive.

Cocktails and Punches

caribbean champagne

Both rum and bananas are naturally associated with the tropics, but wine does not spring so readily to mind when the Caribbean is mentioned. However, remember that France and many Caribbean islands, such as Martinique and Guadeloupe, share a long history.

SERVES 1

½ measure white rum, ½ measure crème de banane,

chilled champagne, to top off, slice of banana, to decorate

1 Pour the rum and crème de banane into a chilled champagne flute. Top off with champagne.

2 Stir gently to mix and decorate with a slice of banana.

"CHAMPAGNE FOR MY SHAM FRIENDS"

AMERICAN FLYER: put 4–6 cracked ice cubes into a cocktail shaker. Pour in 1½ measures white rum, 1 tablespoon lime juice, and ½ teaspoon sugar syrup (see page 9). Shake vigorously until a frost forms. Strain the mixture into a chilled champagne flute and top off with chilled champagne or sparkling white wine.

CHICAGO: rub the rim of a large, chilled brandy glass with a wedge of lemon and then dip in superfine sugar to frost. Put 4–6 cracked ice cubes into a mixing glass. Dash triple sec and Angostura bitters over the ice and pour in 2 measures brandy. Stir and strain into the prepared glass. Top off with chilled champagne or sparkling white wine.

DAWN: pour 1 measure chilled champagne or sparkling white wine, 1 measure chilled dry sherry, and 1 measure chilled lime juice into a chilled cocktail glass. Stir to mix.

polynesian pepper pot

It may seem strange to make a sweet drink and then season it with pepper and spices, but there is a long and honorable culinary tradition of making the most of the slightly acerbic flavor of pineapple in this kind of way.

SERVES 1

4–6 cracked ice cubes, dash of Tabasco sauce, 2 measures vodka,

1 measure golden rum, 4 measures pineapple juice, ½ measure orgeat,

1 tsp lemon juice, ¼ tsp cayenne pepper, pinch of curry powder, to decorate

1 Put the cracked ice into a cocktail shaker. Dash Tabasco sauce over the ice, pour in the vodka, rum, pineapple juice, orgeat, and lemon juice and add the cayenne. Shake vigorously until a frost forms.

2 Strain into a chilled glass and sprinkle curry powder on top.

TOTALLY TROPICAL

POLYNESIAN SOUR: put 4–6 crushed ice cubes into a blender and add 2 measures light rum, ½ measure guava juice, ½ measure lemon juice, and ½ measure orange juice. Blend the mixture until smooth, then pour into a chilled cocktail glass.

POLYNESIA: put 4–6 cracked ice cubes into a cocktail shaker. Dash Angostura bitters over the ice and add 2 measures white rum, 2 measures passion fruit juice, 1 measure lime juice, and 1 egg white. Shake vigorously until a frost forms, then strain into a chilled cocktail glass.

honeymoon

The traditional nuptial journey is so called because the first month of marriage was thought to be sweet—and why not? If you are sick of the sight of champagne following the wedding, why not share this sweet concoction?

SERVES 2

8–10 cracked ice cubes, 4 measures apple brandy,

2 measures Bénédictine, 2 measures lemon juice, 2 tsp triple sec

1 Put the cracked ice cubes into a cocktail shaker. Pour the brandy, Bénédictine, lemon juice, and triple sec over the ice. Shake vigorously until a frost forms.

2 Strain into two chilled cocktail glasses.

WEDDED BLISS

These cocktails all serve one.

BACHELOR'S BAIT: put 4–6 cracked ice cubes into a cocktail shaker. Dash orange bitters over the ice, pour in 2 measures gin and 1 teaspoon grenadine, and add 1 egg white. Shake vigorously until a frost forms, then strain into a chilled cocktail glass.

CUPID: put 4–6 cracked ice cubes into a cocktail shaker. Dash Tabasco sauce over the ice, pour in 2 measures dry sherry and 1 teaspoon sugar syrup (see page 9), and add 1 egg. Shake until a frost forms, then strain into a chilled cocktail glass.

KISS KISS: put 4–6 cracked ice cubes into a mixing glass. Pour 1 measure cherry brandy, 1 measure gin, and 1 measure sweet vermouth over the ice. Stir well, then strain into a chilled cocktail glass.

WEDDING BELLS: put 4–6 cracked ice cubes into a mixing glass. Dash orange bitters over the ice and pour in 2 measures rye whiskey, 1 measure triple sec, and 2 measures Lillet. Stir well to mix, then strain into a chilled cocktail glass.

Nonalcoholic Cocktails

lip smacker

So many delicious ingredients are available today, that nonalcoholic cocktails really have come into their own. This one has all the kick of an alcoholic cocktail.

SERVES 1

4–6 cracked ice cubes, 1 small tomato, peeled, seeded, and chopped, 1 measure orange juice, 2 tsp lime juice, 1 spring onion, chopped, 1 small, fresh red chile, seeded and chopped, pinch of superfine sugar, pinch of salt, dash of Tabasco sauce, slice of lime and a chile rosette (see below), to decorate

1 Put the crushed ice, tomato, orange juice, lime juice, spring onion, and chile in a blender and process until smooth.

2 Pour into a chilled glass, and stir in the sugar, salt, and Tabasco sauce. Decorate with a lime slice and a chile rosette. To make a rosette, use a sharp knife to make 5 or 6 cuts ½ inch from the stalk end to the tip of a long, thin chile. Place in iced water for 30 minutes, until it has fanned out.

OTHER SPICY SHOTS

HOT LIPS: substitute the flesh of ¼ small avocado for the tomato and a seeded and chopped green chile for the red chile.

OPEN PRAIRIE OYSTER: dash Tabasco sauce and white wine vinegar into a wine glass and pour in 1 tsp Worcestershire sauce and 1 measure tomato juice. Stir gently and add 1 egg yolk. Drink down in one, without breaking the egg yolk. (For a Prairie Oyster see page 15.)

DID YOU KNOW?

Sun-ripened tomatoes have a much sweeter and more concentrated flavor than those grown under glass or in polytunnels. Home-grown varieties are best, but those sold on the vine are a good buy.

bloody january

Generally, the best nonalcoholic cocktails are originals rather than pale and often insipid copies of their traditional, alcoholic cousins. This nonalcoholic version of the Bloody Mary is one of the exceptions and has some of the kick of the classic cocktail.

SERVES 1

4–6 crushed ice cubes, 1 medium bell pepper, seeded, and coarsely chopped,

2 large tomatoes, peeled, seeded, and coarsely chopped,

1 fresh green chile, seeded, juice of 1 lime,

salt and freshly ground black pepper, celery stalk, to decorate

1 Put the crushed ice cubes into a blender and add the bell pepper, tomatoes, chile, and lime juice. Blend until smooth.

2 Pour into a chilled highball glass and season to taste with salt and pepper. Decorate with a celery stalk.

VARIATIONS

VIRGIN MARY: put 4–6 cracked ice cubes into a cocktail shaker. Dash Worcestershire sauce and Tabasco sauce over the ice, pour in 4 measures tomato juice and 1 measure lime juice, and add ¼ teaspoon horseradish sauce. Shake vigorously until a frost forms. Strain into a chilled glass and season to taste with salt and freshly ground black pepper. Decorate with a wedge of lime.

FERDINAND THE BULL: put 4–6 cracked ice cubes into a cocktail shaker. Dash Worcestershire sauce and Tabasco sauce over the ice and pour in 4 measures tomato juice, 4 measures chilled bouillon, and 1 measure lime juice. Shake until a frost forms. Half fill a chilled glass with cracked ice cubes and strain the cocktail over them. Season to taste with salt and freshly ground black pepper and decorate with a slice of lime.

(For a Bloody Mary and other alcoholic variations, see page 33.)

carrot cream

Although carrots are vegetables, they have a strong hint of sweetness that makes them or their juice an excellent and delicious basis for mixed drinks. Since raw carrots are packed with vitamins and minerals, they are a healthy option, too.

SERVES 1

4–6 cracked ice cubes, 2 measures carrot juice, 2½ measures light cream,

1 measure orange juice, 1 egg yolk, slice of orange, to decorate

1 Put the cracked ice cubes into a cocktail shaker. Pour the carrot juice, cream, and orange juice over the ice and add the egg yolk. Shake vigorously until a frost forms.

2 Strain into a chilled glass and decorate with the orange slice.

VARIATIONS

CARROT COCKTAIL: put 6–8 crushed ice cubes into a blender and add 3 measures pineapple juice, 2 coarsely chopped small carrots, and ¼ cup crushed pineapple. Blend until slushy. Pour the mixture, without straining, into a chilled glass.

DELIRIOUS DONKEY: put 6–8 crushed ice cubes into a blender and add 3 measures orange juice, 1 coarsely chopped large carrot, and a 2 inch/5 cm piece of peeled and coarsely chopped cucumber. Blend until slushy. Pour, without straining, into a chilled glass and decorate with a slice of cucumber and a slice of orange.

clam digger

This is another good cocktail for a Sunday brunch, when alcoholic drinks can be too soporific and you end up wasting the rest of the day, but you still want something to wake up the taste buds and set them tingling.

SERVES 1

10–12 cracked ice cubes, Tabasco sauce, Worcestershire sauce,

4 measures tomato juice, 4 measures clam juice, ¼ tsp horseradish sauce,

celery salt and freshly ground black pepper,

celery stalk, wedge of lime, to decorate

1 Put 4–6 cracked ice cubes into a cocktail shaker. Dash the Tabasco sauce and Worcestershire sauce over the ice, pour in the tomato juice and clam juice, and add the horseradish sauce. Shake vigorously until a frost forms.

2 Fill a chilled Collins glass with cracked ice cubes and strain the cocktail over them. Season to taste with celery salt and pepper and decorate with a celery stalk and lime wedge.

VARIATIONS

NEW ENGLAND PARTY: put 6–8 crushed ice cubes into a blender and dash Tabasco sauce, Worcestershire sauce, and lemon juice over the ice. Add 1 medium chopped carrot, 2 chopped celery stalks, 1¼ cups tomato juice, and ⅔ cup clam juice. Blend until smooth. Transfer to a pitcher, cover with plastic wrap, and chill in the refrigerator for about 1 hour. Pour the cocktail into 2 chilled glasses and season with salt and freshly ground black pepper to taste. Decorate with cocktail olives speared on a cocktail stick.

BARTENDER'S TIP

A commercial product called Clamato Juice—a mixture of tomato and clam juices—is available from some supermarkets and delicatessens and can be substituted for the separate ingredients.

Cocktails and Punches

eye of the hurricane

In recent years, a vast range of fruit juices and syrups has become widely available. These can extend the range of the cocktail bar and are particularly useful for nonalcoholic mixed drinks, which were once heavily dependent on the somewhat tired old favorites of orange, lemon, and lime juices.

SERVES 1

4–6 cracked ice cubes, 2 measures passion fruit syrup,

1 measure lime juice, bitter lemon, to top off, slice of lemon, to decorate

1 Put the cracked ice cubes into a mixing glass. Pour the syrup and lime juice over the ice and stir well to mix.

2 Strain into a chilled glass and top off with bitter lemon. Stir gently and decorate with the lemon slice.

VARIATIONS

TROPICAL STORM: put 4–6 cracked ice cubes into a cocktail shaker. Pour 2 measures pineapple juice, 2 measures lime juice, 1 measure passion fruit syrup, and ½ teaspoon orgeat over the ice. Shake vigorously until a frost forms. Strain into a small, chilled glass and decorate with a pineapple wedge.

DAYDREAM: half fill a tall, chilled glass with cracked ice cubes. Pour 1½ measures passion fruit syrup over the ice and top off with chilled orange juice. Stir gently to mix and sprinkle with freshly grated nutmeg.

QUIET PASSION: put 4–6 cracked ice cubes into a cocktail shaker. Pour 4 measures grapefruit juice, 4 measures white grape juice, and 1 measure passion fruit juice over the ice. Shake vigorously until a frost forms. Half fill a chilled glass with cracked ice cubes and strain the cocktail over them. Decorate with a slice of lime.

faux kir

A nonalcoholic version of a classic wine cocktail, this drink is just as colorful and tasty. French and Italian fruit syrups are often the best quality and have the most flavor.

SERVES 1

1 measure chilled raspberry syrup, chilled white grape juice, to top off,

twist of lemon peel, to decorate

1 Pour the raspberry syrup into a chilled wine glass. Top off with the grape juice.

2 Stir well to mix and decorate with the lemon twist.

VARIATIONS

FAUX KIR ROYALE: put 4–6 cracked ice cubes into a mixing glass. Pour 1½ measures raspberry syrup over the ice. Stir well to mix, then strain into a wine glass. Top off with chilled sparkling apple juice and stir.

KNICKS VICTORY COOLER: half fill a tall, chilled glass with cracked ice cubes. Pour 2 measures apricot juice over the ice, top off with raspberry soda, and stir gently. Decorate with a spiral of orange peel and fresh raspberries.

COCOBERRY: rub ½ cup raspberries through a metal strainer with the back of a spoon and transfer the purée to a blender. Add 4–6 crushed ice cubes, 1 measure coconut cream, and ²/₃ cup pineapple juice. Blend until smooth, then pour the mixture, without straining, into a chilled glass. Decorate with pineapple wedges and fresh raspberries.

ALL SHOOK UP: put ½ cup mixed strawberries and raspberries, 4 measures chilled milk, 4 measures chilled plain yogurt, and 1 teaspoon rosewater into a blender. Blend until smooth and then pour the mixture into a chilled glass. Stir in ½ teaspoon clear honey and decorate with a strawberry and a raspberry. Serve with straws.

BARTENDER'S TIP

For a Kir and other alcoholic variations, see page 39.

Cocktails and Punches

juicy julep

Taken from the Arabic word, meaning a rose syrup, it seems likely that this was always intended to be a nonalcoholic drink and that it was bourbon-drinkers who hijacked the term, not the other way around. (For a Mint Julep and other alcoholic variations, see page 17.)

SERVES 1

4–6 cracked ice cubes, 1 measure orange juice, 1 measure pineapple juice, 1 measure lime juice, ½ measure raspberry syrup, 4 crushed fresh mint leaves, ginger ale, to top off, sprig of fresh mint, to decorate

1 Put the cracked ice cubes into a cocktail shaker. Pour the orange juice, pineapple juice, lime juice, and raspberry syrup over the ice and add the mint leaves. Shake vigorously until a frost forms.

2 Strain into a chilled Collins glass, top off with ginger ale, and stir gently. Decorate with a fresh mint sprig.

OTHER JUNIOR RELATIVES

SALTY PUPPY: mix equal quantities of granulated sugar and coarse salt on a saucer. Rub the rim of a small, chilled glass with a wedge of lime, then dip in the sugar/salt mixture to frost. Fill the glass with cracked ice cubes and pour ½ measure lime juice over them. Top off with grapefruit juice.

BABY BELLINI: pour 2 measures peach juice and 1 measure lemon juice into a chilled champagne flute and stir well. Top off with sparkling apple juice and stir.

COOL COLLINS: put 6 fresh mint leaves into a tall, chilled glass and add 1 teaspoon superfine sugar and 2 measures lemon juice. Crush the leaves with a spoon until the sugar has dissolved. Fill the glass with cracked ice cubes and top off with sparkling water. Stir gently and decorate with a fresh mint sprig and a slice of lemon. (For a Tom Collins and other alcoholic variations, see page 22.)

island cooler

Nothing could be more refreshing on a hot summer's day than this colorful combination of tropical fruit juices. To get into a party mood, go to town with the decoration with a cocktail parasol, swizzle stick, and straws, as well as fresh fruit, if you like.

SERVES 1

8–10 cracked ice cubes, 2 measures orange juice, 1 measure lemon juice,

1 measure pineapple juice, 1 measure papaya juice,

½ tsp grenadine, sparkling mineral water, to top off,

pineapple wedges, cocktail cherries, to decorate

1 Put 4–6 cracked ice cubes into a cocktail shaker. Pour the orange juice, lemon juice, pineapple juice, papaya juice, and grenadine over the ice. Shake vigorously until a frost forms.

2 Half fill a chilled Collins glass with cracked ice cubes and pour the cocktail over them. Top off with sparkling mineral water and stir gently. Decorate with pineapple wedges and cocktail cherries speared on a cocktail stick.

ANOTHER EXOTIC DESTINATION

CARIBBEAN COCKTAIL: put 4–6 crushed ice cubes into a blender and add a dash of lime juice, 4 measures orange juice, the coarsely chopped flesh of ½ mango, and ½ peeled and sliced banana. Blend until smooth. Half fill a chilled glass with cracked ice cubes and pour the cocktail over them. Decorate with a slice of lime.

DID YOU KNOW?

Papaya seeds, although edible, have a very peppery flavor so, if you are squeezing the juice yourself, it is important to remove all of them. Papaya juice is commercially available.

Cocktails and Punches

little prince

Sparkling apple juice is a particularly useful ingredient in nonalcoholic cocktails because it adds flavor and color, as well as fizz. Try using it as a substitute for champagne in nonalcoholic versions of such cocktails as Buck's Fizz (see page 41).

SERVES 1

4–6 cracked ice cubes, 1 measure apricot juice, 1 measure lemon juice,

2 measures sparkling apple juice, twist of lemon peel, to decorate

1 Put the cracked ice cubes into a mixing glass. Pour the apricot juice, lemon juice, and apple juice over the ice and stir well.

2 Strain into a chilled highball glass and decorate with the lemon twist.

AN APPLE A DAY

APPLE FRAZZLE: put 4–6 cracked ice cubes into a cocktail shaker. Pour 4 measures apple juice, 1 teaspoon sugar syrup (see page 9), and ½ teaspoon lemon juice over the ice. Shake vigorously until a frost forms. Strain into a chilled glass and top off with sparkling mineral water.

BITE OF THE APPLE: put 4–6 crushed ice cubes into a blender and add 5 measures apple juice, 1 measure lime juice, ½ teaspoon orgeat, and 1 tablespoon apple sauce or apple purée. Blend until smooth, then pour into a chilled glass. Sprinkle with ground cinnamon.

PROHIBITION PUNCH (to serve 25): pour 3¾ cups apple juice, 1½ cups lemon juice, and ½ cup sugar syrup (see page 9) into a large pitcher. Add cracked ice cubes and 9 cups ginger ale. Stir gently to mix. Serve in chilled glasses, decorated with slices of orange and with straws.

RED APPLE SUNSET: put 4–6 cracked ice cubes into a cocktail shaker. Dash grenadine over the ice and pour in 2 measures apple juice and 2 measures grapefruit juice. Shake vigorously until a frost forms. Strain into a chilled cocktail glass.

sparkling peach melba

Peach Melba was a dessert invented by Escoffier, chef at the Savoy Hotel in London, in honor of the Australian opera singer Dame Nellie Melba. This simple, but perfect partnership of peaches and raspberries has become a classic combination, now transformed into a wonderfully refreshing cocktail.

SERVES 1

¼ cup frozen raspberries, 4 measures peach juice, sparkling mineral water, to top off

1 Rub the raspberries through a wire strainer with the back of a wooden spoon. Transfer the purée to a cocktail shaker.

2 Pour the peach juice into the cocktail shaker and shake vigorously until a frost forms.

3 Strain into a tall, chilled glass and top off with sparkling mineral water. Stir gently.

LIFE'S A PEACH

PEACHY MELBA: put 4–6 cracked ice cubes into a cocktail shaker. Pour 3 measures peach juice, 1 measure lemon juice, 1 measure lime juice, and 1 measure grenadine over the ice. Shake until a frost forms. Strain into a small, chilled glass and decorate with a slice of peach.

UNDER THE BOARDWALK: put 4–6 crushed ice cubes into a blender. Add 2 measures lemon juice, ½ teaspoon sugar syrup (see page 9), and ½ peeled and chopped peach. Blend until slushy, then pour into a chilled glass. Top off with sparkling mineral water and stir gently. Decorate with raspberries.

PEACHY CREAM: put 4–6 cracked ice cubes into a cocktail shaker. Pour 2 measures peach juice and 2 measures light cream into a cocktail shaker. Shake vigorously until a frost forms. Half fill a small, chilled glass with cracked ice cubes and then strain the cocktail over them.

BARTENDER'S TIP

Using frozen raspberries ensures a convenient supply at any time of year. If you prefer to use fresh raspberries, put 4–6 crushed ice cubes into the cocktail shaker before adding the purée.

california smoothie

Smoothies of all sorts—alcoholic and nonalcoholic—have become immensely popular in the last two or three years. The secret of success is to blend them on medium speed until just smooth.

SERVES 1

1 banana, peeled and thinly sliced, ½ cup strawberries,

½ cup pitted dates, 4½ tsp honey,

1 cup orange juice, 4–6 crushed ice cubes

1 Put the banana, strawberries, dates, and honey into a blender and blend until smooth.

2 Add the orange juice and crushed ice cubes and blend again until smooth. Pour into a chilled Collins glass.

SMOOTH AS SILK

APRICOT SMOOTHIE: put 4–6 crushed ice cubes into a blender. Add 2 peeled, pitted, and chopped apricots, 2 measures pineapple juice, 1 measure lime juice, and 1 measure cherry syrup. Blend until smooth, then pour into a chilled glass.

MANGO SMOOTHIE: put 4–6 crushed ice cubes into a blender and add 1 measure lime juice, 1 small, peeled, pitted, and chopped mango, and 2 hulled strawberries. Blend until smooth, then pour into a chilled goblet. Decorate with a strawberry and a slice of lime.

PAPAYA SMOOTHIE: put 4–6 crushed ice cubes into a blender and add 3/4 cup orange juice, 1 peeled and sliced banana, ½ peeled and diced papaya, 1½ teaspoons clear honey, and ¼ teaspoon vanilla extract. Blend until smooth, then pour into a chilled glass.

PINEAPPLE SMOOTHIE: put 4–6 crushed ice cubes into a blender and add 2 measures pineapple juice, 1 measure lime juice, and ½ banana. Blend until smooth, then pour the mixture into a chilled glass.

italian soda

Available from Italian delicatessens and some supermarkets, Italian syrup comes in a wide variety of flavors, including a range of fruit and nuts. French syrups are similar and also include many different flavors. You can substitute your favorite for the hazelnut used here and vary the quantity depending on how sweet and syrupy you like your drinks.

SERVES 1

6–8 cracked ice cubes, 1–1½ measures hazelnut syrup,

sparkling mineral water, to top off, slice of lime, to decorate

1 Fill a chilled Collins glass with cracked ice cubes. Pour the hazelnut syrup over the ice and top off with sparkling mineral water.

2 Stir gently and decorate with the lime slice.

VARIATIONS

HEAVENLY DAYS: put 4–6 cracked ice cubes into a cocktail shaker. Pour 2 measures hazelnut syrup, 2 measures lemon juice, and 1 teaspoon grenadine over the ice. Shake vigorously until a frost forms. Half fill a glass with cracked ice cubes and strain the cocktail over them. Top off with sparkling mineral water. Stir gently and then decorate with a slice of orange.

CHERRY STONE: put 4–6 cracked ice cubes into a cocktail shaker. Pour 2 measures cherry syrup and 2 measures lime juice over the ice. Shake vigorously until a frost forms. Half fill a glass with cracked ice cubes and strain the cocktail over them. Top off with sparkling apple juice. Stir gently and decorate with cocktail cherries.

ORGEAT COLA: put 4–6 cracked ice cubes into a cocktail shaker. Pour 2 measures orgeat and 2 measures lime juice over the ice. Shake vigorously until a frost forms. Half fill a glass with cracked ice cubes and strain the cocktail over them. Top off with cola. Stir gently and decorate with a pineapple wedge.

Cocktails and Punches

grapefruit cooler

This is a wonderfully refreshing drink that is ideal for serving at a family barbecue. Start making this at least two hours before you want to serve it to have plenty of time for the mint to steep in the syrup.

SERVES 6

2 oz/60 g fresh mint, 2 measures sugar syrup (see page 9),

2 cups grapefruit juice, 4 measures lemon juice, about 30 cracked ice cubes,

sparkling mineral water, to top off, sprigs of fresh mint, to decorate

1 Crush the fresh mint leaves and place in a small bowl. Add the sugar syrup and stir well. Set aside for at least 2 hours to soak, mashing the mint with a spoon from time to time.

2 Strain the syrup into a pitcher and add the grapefruit juice and lemon juice. Cover with plastic wrap and chill in the refrigerator for at least 2 hours.

3 To serve, fill six chilled Collins glasses with cracked ice. Divide the cocktail among the glasses and top off with sparkling mineral water. Decorate with fresh mint sprigs.

COOL IT

COCONUT COOLER: put 4–6 cracked ice cubes into a cocktail shaker. Pour 2 measures coconut milk and 2 measures lime juice over the ice and shake until a frost forms. Half fill a chilled glass with cracked ice cubes and then strain the cocktail over them. Decorate with a sprig of fresh mint.

cranberry punch

A sophisticated, nonalcoholic punch, this can also be served hot for a winter party—it is especially good for celebrating the New Year—as well as chilled in the summer.

SERVES 10

2½ cups cranberry juice, 2½ cups orange juice,

⅔ cup water, ½ tsp ground ginger, ¼ tsp ground cinnamon,

¼ tsp freshly grated nutmeg, cracked ice cubes or block of ice, optional,

fresh cranberries, 1 egg white, lightly beaten,

superfine sugar, sprigs of fresh mint, to decorate cold punch,

slices of lemon, slices of orange, to decorate hot punch

1 First prepare the decoration, if you are planning to serve the punch cold. Dip the cranberries, one by one, in the egg white and let the excess drip off, then roll them in the sugar to frost, shaking off any excess. Set aside on baking parchment to dry. Brush the mint leaves with egg white and then dip in the sugar to frost, shaking off any excess. Set aside on baking parchment to dry.

2 Put the cranberry juice, orange juice, water, ginger, cinnamon, and nutmeg in a pan and bring to a boil. Lower the heat and simmer for 5 minutes.

3 Remove the pan from the heat. If serving hot, ladle into warmed individual punch glasses or pour into a warmed punch bowl. Decorate with slices of lemon and orange.

4 If serving the punch cold, set aside to cool, then pour into a pitcher, cover with plastic wrap, and chill in the refrigerator for at least 2 hours, until required.

5 To serve the cold punch, place cracked ice or a block of ice in a chilled punch bowl and pour in the punch. Alternatively, fill glasses with cracked ice and then pour the punch over them. Decorate with the frosted cranberries and mint leaves.

mocha slush

Definitely for people with a sweet tooth, this is a chocoholic's dream and is popular with adults, as well as children.

SERVES 1

4–6 crushed ice cubes, 2 measures coffee syrup, 1 measure chocolate syrup,

4 measures milk, grated chocolate, to decorate

1 Put the crushed ice cubes into a blender and add the coffee syrup, chocolate syrup, and milk. Blend until slushy.

2 Pour into a chilled goblet and sprinkle with grated chocolate.

SWEET DREAMS

CHOCOMINT SLUSH: put 4–6 crushed ice cubes into a blender and add 2 measures chocolate syrup, 1 measure peppermint syrup, and 4 measures milk. Blend until slushy. Pour the mixture into a chilled goblet. Decorate with a sprig of fresh mint.

CHOCOLATE CHAMPERS: pour 1½ measures chocolate syrup into a tall, chilled glass. Add 3½ measures chilled milk and stir well to mix. Top off with club soda and stir vigorously.

ALEXANDER'S DAUGHTER: put 4–6 cracked ice cubes into a cocktail shaker. Pour 1 measure chocolate syrup, 1 measure ginger syrup, and 1 measure light cream over the ice. Shake vigorously until a frost forms, then strain the mixture into a chilled cocktail glass. Sprinkle with freshly ground nutmeg. (For an Alexander and other alcoholic variations, see page 21).

BLACK FOREST: pour 1 measure chocolate syrup into a small, chilled glass, such as a sherry or liqueur glass. Pour 1 measure cherry syrup on top and then pour in 1 measure heavy cream.

shirley temple

This is one of the most famous of classic nonalcoholic cocktails. Shirley Temple Black became a respected diplomat, but this cocktail dates from the days when she was an immensely popular child movie star in the 1930s.

SERVES 1

8–10 cracked ice cubes, 2 measures lemon juice, ½ measure grenadine,
½ measure sugar syrup (see page 9), ginger ale, to top off,
slice of orange, cocktail cherry, to decorate

1 Put 4–6 cracked ice cubes into a cocktail shaker. Pour the lemon juice, grenadine, and sugar syrup over the ice and shake vigorously.

2 Half fill a small, chilled glass with cracked ice cubes and strain the cocktail over them. Top off with ginger ale. Decorate with an orange slice and a cocktail cherry.

OTHER CLASSICS

ST. CLEMENTS: put 6–8 cracked ice cubes into a chilled glass. Pour 2 measures orange juice and 2 measures bitter lemon over the ice. Stir gently and decorate with a slice of orange and a slice of lemon.

BLACK AND TAN: pour ⅔ cup chilled ginger ale into a chilled glass. Add ⅔ cup chilled ginger beer. Do not stir. Decorate with a wedge of lime.

TEA PUNCH: put 4–6 cracked ice cubes into a mixing glass. Pour 3 measures cold black tea, 3 measures orange juice, 3 measures sparkling apple juice, and 1½ measures lemon juice over the ice. Stir well to mix, then pour into a tall, chilled glass. Decorate with a lemon slice.

BEACHCOMBER: put 4–6 cracked ice cubes into a cocktail shaker. Pour ⅔ cup guava juice, 2 measures lime juice, and 1 measure raspberry syrup over the ice. Shake vigorously until a frost forms, then pour into a chilled glass.